The Pelican

General Editors

STEPHEN ORGEL

A. R. BRAUNMULLER

Titus Andronicus

Ira Aldridge as Aaron the Moor, c. 1835

William Shakespeare

———

Titus Andronicus

EDITED BY RUSS McDONALD

PENGUIN BOOKS

PENGUIN BOOKS

Published by the Penguin Group
Penguin Putnam Inc., 375 Hudson Street,
New York, New York 10014, U.S.A.
Penguin Books Ltd, 27 Wrights Lane,
London W8 5TZ, England
Penguin Books Australia Ltd, Ringwood,
Victoria, Australia
Penguin Books Canada Ltd, 10 Alcorn Avenue,
Toronto, Ontario, Canada M4V 3B2
Penguin Books (N.Z.) Ltd, 182–190 Wairau Road,
Auckland 10, New Zealand

Penguin Books Ltd, Registered Offices:
Harmondsworth, Middlesex, England

Titus Andronicus edited by Gustav Cross published in the
United States of America in Penguin Books 1966
Revised edition published 1977
This new edition edited by Russ McDonald published 2000

1 3 5 7 9 10 8 6 4 2

ISBN 0-14-07.1491-X

Printed in the United States of America
Set in Garamond
Designed by Virginia Norey

Contents

Publisher's Note

IT IS ALMOST half a century since the first volumes of the
Pelican Shakespeare appeared under the general editorship
of Alfred Harbage. The fact that a new edition, rather
than simply a revision, has been undertaken reflects the
profound changes textual and critical studies of Shakespeare have undergone in the past twenty years. For the
new Pelican series, the texts of the plays and poems have
been thoroughly revised in accordance with recent scholarship, and in some cases have been entirely reedited. New
introductions and notes have been provided in all the volumes. But the new Shakespeare is also designed as a successor to the original series; the previous editions have
been taken into account, and the advice of the previous
editors has been solicited where it was feasible to do so.

Certain textual features of the new Pelican Shakespeare
should be particularly noted. All lines are numbered that
contain a word, phrase, or allusion explained in the
glossarial notes. In addition, for convenience, every tenth
line is also numbered, in italics when no annotation is indicated. The intrusive and often inaccurate place headings
inserted by early editors are omitted (as is becoming standard practice), but for the convenience of those who miss
them, an indication of locale now appears as the first item
in the annotation of each scene.

In the interest of both elegance and utility, each speech
prefix is set in a separate line when the speaker's lines are
in verse, except when those words form the second half of
a verse line. Thus the verse form of the speech is kept vi-
sually intact. What is printed as verse and what is printed
as prose has, in general, the authority of the original texts.
Departures from the original texts in this regard have only
the authority of editorial tradition and the judgment of
the Pelican editors; and, in a few instances, are admittedly
arbitrary.

The Theatrical World

Economic realities determined the theatrical world in which Shakespeare's plays were written, performed, and received. For centuries in England, the primary theatrical tradition was nonprofessional. Craft guilds (or "mysteries") provided religious drama – mystery plays – as part of the celebration of religious and civic festivals, and schools and universities staged classical and neoclassical drama in both Latin and English as part of their curricula. In these forms, drama was established and socially acceptable. Professional theater, in contrast, existed on the margins of society. The acting companies were itinerant; playhouses could be any available space – the great halls of the aristocracy, town squares, civic halls, inn yards, fair booths, or open fields – and income was sporadic, dependent on the passing of the hat or on the bounty of local patrons. The actors, moreover, were considered little better than vagabonds, constantly in danger of arrest or expulsion.

In the late 1560s and 1570s, however, English professional theater began to gain respectability. Wealthy aristocrats fond of drama – the Lord Admiral, for example, or the Lord Chamberlain – took acting companies under their protection so that the players technically became members of their households and were no longer subject to arrest as homeless or masterless men. Permanent theaters were first built at this time as well, allowing the companies to control and charge for entry to their performances.

Shakespeare's livelihood, and the stunning artistic explosion in which he participated, depended on pragmatic and architectural effort. Professional theater requires ways to restrict access to its offerings; if it does not, and admission fees cannot be charged, the actors do not get paid, the costumes go to a pawnbroker, and there is no such thing as a professional, ongoing theatrical tradition. The answer to that economic need arrived in the late 1560s and 1570s with the creation of the so-called public or amphitheater playhouse. Recent discoveries indicate that the precursor of the Globe playhouse in London (where Shakespeare's mature plays were presented) and the Rose theater (which presented Christopher Marlowe's plays and some of Shakespeare's earliest ones) was the Red Lion theater of 1567. Archaeological studies of the foundations of the Rose and Globe theaters have revealed that the open-air theater of the 1590s and later was probably a polygonal building with fourteen to twenty or twenty-four sides, multistoried, from 75 to 100 feet in diameter, with a raised, partly covered "thrust" stage that projected into a group of standing patrons, or "groundlings," and a covered gallery, seating up to 2,500 or more (very crowded) spectators.

These theaters might have been about half full on any given day, though the audiences were larger on holidays or when a play was advertised, as old and new were, through printed playbills posted around London. The metropolitan area's late-Tudor, early-Stuart population (circa 1590–1620) has been estimated at about 150,000 to 250,000. It has been supposed that in the mid-1590s there were about 15,000 spectators per week at the public theaters; thus, as many as 10 percent of the local population went to the theater regularly. Consequently, the theaters' repertories – the plays available for this experienced and frequent audience – had to change often: in the month between September 15 and October 15, 1595, for instance, the Lord Admiral's Men performed twenty-eight times in eighteen different plays.

Since natural light illuminated the amphitheaters' stages, performances began between noon and two o'clock and ran without a break for two or three hours. They often concluded with a jig, a fencing display, or some other nondramatic exhibition. Weather conditions determined the season for the amphitheaters: plays were performed every day (including Sundays, sometimes, to clerical dismay) except during Lent – the forty days before Easter – or periods of plague, or sometimes during the summer months when law courts were not in session and the most affluent members of the audience were not in London.

To a modern theatergoer, an amphitheater stage like that of the Rose or Globe would appear an unfamiliar mixture of plainness and elaborate decoration. Much of the structure was carved or painted, sometimes to imitate marble; elsewhere, as under the canopy projecting over the stage, to represent the stars and the zodiac. Appropriate painted canvas pictures (of Jerusalem, for example, if the play was set in that city) were apparently hung on the wall behind the acting area, and tragedies were accompanied by black hangings, presumably something like crepe festoons or bunting. Although these theaters did not employ what we would call scenery, early modern spectators saw numerous large props, such as the "bar" at which a prisoner stood during a trial, the "mossy bank" where lovers reclined, an arbor for amorous conversation, a chariot, gallows, tables, trees, beds, thrones, writing desks, and so forth. Audiences might learn a scene's location from a sign (reading "Athens," for example) carried across the stage (as in Bertolt Brecht's twentieth-century productions). Equally captivating (and equally irritating to the theater's enemies) were the rich costumes and personal props the actors used: the most valuable items in the surviving theatrical inventories are the swords, gowns, robes, crowns, and other items worn or carried by the performers.

Magic appealed to Shakespeare's audiences as much as it does to us today, and the theater exploited many deceptive and spectacular devices. A winch in the loft above the stage, called "the heavens," could lower and raise actors playing gods, goddesses, and other supernatural figures to and from the main acting area, just as one or more trap-doors permitted entrances and exits to and from the area, called "hell," beneath the stage. Actors wore elementary makeup such as wigs, false beards, and face paint, and they employed pig's bladders filled with animal blood to make wounds seem more real. They had rudimentary but effective ways of pretending to behead or hang a person. Supernumeraries (stagehands or actors not needed in a particular scene) could make thunder sounds (by shaking a metal sheet or rolling an iron ball down a chute) and show lightning (by blowing inflammable resin through tubes into a flame). Elaborate fireworks enhanced the effects of dragons flying through the air or imitated such celestial phenomena as comets, shooting stars, and multiple suns. Horses' hoofbeats, bells (located perhaps in the tower above the stage), trumpets and drums, clocks, cannon shots and gunshots, and the like were common sound effects. And the music of viols, cornets, oboes, and recorders was a regular feature of theatrical performances.

For two relatively brief spans, from the late 1570s to 1590 and from 1599 to 1614, the amphitheaters competed with the so-called private, or indoor, theaters, which originated as, or later represented themselves as, educational institutions training boys as singers for church services and court performances. These indoor theaters had two features that were distinct from the amphitheaters': their personnel and their playing spaces. The amphitheaters' adult companies included both adult men, who played the male roles, and boys, who played the female roles; the private, or indoor, theater companies, on the other hand, were entirely composed of boys aged about 8 to 16, who were, or could pretend to be, candidates for singers in a church or a royal boys' choir. (Until 1660, professional theatrical companies included no women.) The playing space would appear much more familiar to modern audiences than the long-vanished amphitheaters; the later indoor theaters were, in fact, the ancestors of the typical modern theater. They were enclosed spaces, usually rectangular, with the stage filling one end of the rectangle and the audience arrayed in seats or benches across (and sometimes lining) the building's longer axis. These spaces staged plays less frequently than the public theaters (perhaps only once a week) and held far fewer spectators than the amphitheaters: about 200 to 600, as opposed to 2,500 or more. Fewer patrons mean a smaller gross income, unless each pays more. Not surprisingly, then, private theaters charged higher prices than the amphitheaters, probably sixpence, as opposed to a penny for the cheapest entry.

Protected from the weather, the indoor theaters presented plays later in the day than the amphitheaters, and used artificial illumination – candles in sconces or candelabra. But candles melt, and need replacing, snuffing, and trimming, and these practical requirements may have been part of the reason the indoor theaters introduced breaks in the performance, the intermission so dear to the heart of theatergoers and to the pocketbooks of theater concessionaires ever since. Whether motivated by the need to tend to the candles or by the entrepreneurs' wishing to sell oranges and liquor, or both, the indoor theaters eventually established the modern convention of the noncontinuous performance. In the early modern "private" theater, musical performances apparently filled the intermissions, which in Stuart theater jargon seem to have been called "acts."

At the end of the first decade of the seventeenth century, the distinction between public amphitheaters and private indoor companies ceased. For various cultural, political, and economic reasons, individual companies gained control of both the public, open-air theaters and the indoor ones, and companies mixing adult men and boys took over the formerly "private" theaters. Despite the death of the boys' companies and of their highly innovative theaters (for which such luminous playwrights as Ben Jonson, George Chapman, and John Marston wrote), their playing spaces and conventions had an immense impact on subsequent plays: not merely for the intervals (which stressed the artistic and architectonic importance of "acts"), but also because they introduced political and social satire as a popular dramatic ingredient, even in tragedy, and a wider range of actorly effects, encouraged by their more intimate playing spaces.

Even the briefest sketch of the Shakespearean theatrical world would be incomplete without some comment on the social and cultural dimensions of theaters and playing in the period. In an intensely hierarchical and status-conscious society, professional actors and their ventures had hardly any respectability; as we have indicated, to protect themselves against laws designed to curb vagabondage and the increase of masterless men, actors resorted to the near-fiction that they were the servants of noble masters, and wore their distinctive livery. Hence the company for which Shakespeare wrote in the 1590s called itself the Lord Chamberlain's Men and pretended that the public, money-getting performances were in fact rehearsals for private performances before that high court official. From 1598, the Privy Council had licensed theatrical companies, and after 1603, with the accession of King James I, the companies gained explicit royal protection, just as the Queen's Men had for a time under Queen Elizabeth. The Chamberlain's Men became the King's Men, and the other companies were patronized by the other members of the royal family.

These designations were legal fictions that half-concealed an important economic and social development, the evolution away from the theater's organization on the model of the guild, a self-regulating confraternity of individual artisans, into a proto-capitalist organization. Shakespeare's company became a joint-stock company, where persons who supplied capital and, in some cases, such as Shakespeare's, capital and talent, employed themselves and others in earning a return on that capital. This development meant that actors and theater companies were outside both the traditional guild structures, which required some form of civic or royal charter, and the feudal household organization of master-and-servant. This anomalous, maverick social and economic condition made theater companies practically unruly and potentially even dangerous; consequently, numerous official bodies – including the London metropolitan and ecclesiastical authorities as well as, occasionally, the royal court itself – tried, without much success, to control and even to disband them.

Public officials had good reason to want to close the theaters: they were attractive nuisances – they drew often riotous crowds, they were always noisy, and they could be politically offensive and socially insubordinate. Until the Civil War, however, anti-theatrical forces failed to shut down professional theater, for many reasons – limited surveillance and few police powers, tensions or outright hostilities among the agencies that sought to check or channel theatrical activity, and lack of clear policies for control. Another reason must have been the theaters' undeniable popularity. Curtailing any activity enjoyed by such a substantial percentage of the population was difficult, as various Roman emperors attempting to limit circuses had learned, and the Tudor-Stuart audience was not merely large, it was socially diverse and included women. The prevalence of public entertainment in this period has been underestimated. In fact, fairs, holidays, games, sporting events, the equivalent of modern parades, freak shows, and street exhibitions all abounded, but the theater was the most widely and frequently available entertainment to which people of every class had access. That fact helps account both for its quantity and for the fear and anger it aroused.

William Shakespeare of Stratford-upon-Avon, Gentleman

Many people have said that we know very little about William Shakespeare's life – pinheads and postcards are often mentioned as appropriately tiny surfaces on which to record the available information. More imaginatively and perhaps more correctly, Ralph Waldo Emerson wrote, "Shakespeare is the only biographer of Shakespeare. . . . So far from Shakespeare's being the least known, he is the one person in all modern history fully known to us."

In fact, we know more about Shakespeare's life than we do about almost any other English writer's of his era. His last will and testament (dated March 25, 1616) survives, as do numerous legal contracts and court documents involving Shakespeare as principal or witness, and parish records in Stratford and London. Shakespeare appears quite often in official records of King James's royal court, and of course Shakespeare's name appears on numerous title pages and in the written and recorded words of his literary contemporaries Robert Greene, Henry Chettle, Francis Meres, John Davies of Hereford, Ben Jonson, and many others. Indeed, if we make due allowance for the bloating of modern, run-of-the-mill bureaucratic records, more information has survived over the past four hundred years about William Shakespeare of Stratford-upon-Avon, Warwickshire, than is likely to survive in the next four hundred years about any reader of these words.

What we do not have are entire categories of information – Shakespeare's private letters or diaries, drafts and revisions of poems and plays, critical prefaces or essays, commendatory verse for other writers' works, or instructions guiding his fellow actors in their performances, for instance – that we imagine would help us understand and appreciate his surviving writings. For all we know, many such data never existed as written records. Many literary and theatrical critics, not knowing what might once have existed, more or less cheerfully accept the situation; some even make a theoretical virtue of it by claiming that such data are irrelevant to understanding and interpreting the plays and poems.

So, what do we know about William Shakespeare, the man responsible for thirty-seven or perhaps more plays, more than 150 sonnets, two lengthy narrative poems, and some shorter poems?

While many families by the name of Shakespeare (or some variant spelling) can be identified in the English Midlands as far back as the twelfth century, it seems likely that the dramatist's grandfather, Richard, moved to Snitterfield, a town not far from Stratford-upon-Avon, sometime before 1529. In Snitterfield, Richard Shakespeare leased farmland from the very wealthy Robert Arden. By 1552, Richard's son John had moved to a large house on Henley Street in Stratford-upon-Avon, the house that stands today as "The Birthplace." In Stratford, John Shakespeare traded as a glover, dealt in wool, and lent money at interest; he also served in a variety of civic posts, including "High Bailiff," the municipality's equivalent of mayor. In 1557, he married Robert Arden's youngest daughter, Mary. Mary and John had four sons – William was the oldest – and four daughters, of whom only Joan outlived her most celebrated sibling. William was baptized (an event entered in the Stratford parish church records) on April 26, 1564, and it has become customary, without any good factual support, to suppose he was born on April 23, which happens to be the feast day of Saint George, patron saint of England, and is also the date on which he died, in 1616. Shakespeare married Anne Hathaway in 1582, when he was eighteen and she was twenty-six; their first child was born five months later. It has been generally assumed that the marriage was enforced and subsequently unhappy, but these are only assumptions; it has been estimated, for instance, that up to one third of Elizabethan brides were pregnant when they married. Anne and William Shakespeare had three children: Susanna, who married a prominent local physician, John Hall; and the twins Hamnet, who died young in 1596, and Judith, who married Thomas Quiney – apparently a rather shady individual. The name Hamnet was unusual but not unique: he and his twin sister were named for their godparents, Shakespeare's neighbors Hamnet and Judith Sadler. Shakespeare's father died in 1601 (the year of *Hamlet*), and Mary Arden Shakespeare died in 1608 (the year of *Coriolanus*). William Shakespeare's last surviving direct descendant was his granddaughter Elizabeth Hall, who died in 1670.

Between the birth of the twins in 1585 and a clear reference to Shakespeare as a practicing London dramatist in Robert Greene's sensationalizing, satiric pamphlet, *Greene's Groatsworth of Wit* (1592), there is no record of where William Shakespeare was or what he was doing. These seven so-called lost years have been imaginatively filled by scholars and other students of Shakespeare: some think he traveled to Italy, or fought in the Low Countries, or studied law or medicine, or worked as an apprentice actor/writer, and so on to even more fanciful possibilities. Whatever the biographical facts for those "lost" years, Greene's nasty remarks in 1592 testify to professional envy and to the fact that Shakespeare already had a successful career in London. Speaking to his fellow playwrights, Greene warns both generally and specifically:

> . . . trust them [actors] not: for there is an upstart crow, beautified with our feathers, that with his tiger's heart wrapped in a player's hide supposes he is as well able to bombast out a blank verse as the best of you; and being an absolute Johannes Factotum, is in his own conceit the only Shake-scene in a country.

The passage mimics a line from *3 Henry VI* (hence the play must have been performed before Greene wrote) and seems to say that "Shake-scene" is both actor and play-wright, a jack-of-all-trades. That same year, Henry Chettle protested Greene's remarks in *Kind-Heart's Dream,* and each of the next two years saw the publication of poems – *Venus and Adonis* and *The Rape of Lucrece,* respectively – publicly ascribed to (and dedicated by) Shakespeare. Early in 1595 he was named one of the senior members of a prominent acting company, the Lord Chamberlain's Men, when they received payment for court performances during the 1594 Christmas season.

Clearly, Shakespeare had achieved both success and reputation in London. In 1596, upon Shakespeare's application, the College of Arms granted his father the now-familiar coat of arms he had taken the first steps to obtain almost twenty years before, and in 1598, John's son – now permitted to call himself "gentleman" – took a 10 percent share in the new Globe playhouse. In 1597, he bought a substantial bourgeois house, called New Place, in Stratford – the garden remains, but Shakespeare's house, several times rebuilt, was torn down in 1759 – and over the next few years Shakespeare spent large sums buying land and making other investments in the town and its environs. Though he worked in London, his family remained in Stratford, and he seems always to have considered Stratford the home he would eventually return to. Something approaching a disinterested appreciation of Shakespeare's popular and professional status appears in Francis Meres's *Palladis Tamia* (1598), a not especially imaginative and perhaps therefore persuasive record of literary reputations. Reviewing contemporary English writers, Meres lists the titles of many of Shakespeare's plays, including one not now known, *Love's Labor's Won,* and praises his "mellifluous & hony-tongued" "sugred Sonnets," which were then circulating in manuscript (they were first collected in 1609). Meres describes Shakespeare as "one of the best" English playwrights of both comedy and tragedy. In *Remains . . . Concerning Britain* (1605),

William Camden – a more authoritative source than the imitative Meres – calls Shakespeare one of the "most pregnant witts of these our times" and joins him with such writers as Chapman, Daniel, Jonson, Marston, and Spenser. During the first decades of the seventeenth century, publishers began to attribute numerous play quartos, including some non-Shakespearean ones, to Shakespeare, either by name or initials, and we may assume that they deemed Shakespeare's name and supposed authorship, true or false, commercially attractive.

For the next ten years or so, various records show Shakespeare's dual career as playwright and man of the theater in London, and as an important local figure in Stratford. In 1608-9 his acting company – designated the "King's Men" soon after King James had succeeded Queen Elizabeth in 1603 – rented, refurbished, and opened a small interior playing space, the Blackfriars theater, in London, and Shakespeare was once again listed as a substantial sharer in the group of proprietors of the playhouse. By May 11, 1612, however, he describes himself as a Stratford resident in a London lawsuit – an indication that he had withdrawn from day-to-day professional activity and returned to the town where he had always had his main financial interests. When Shakespeare bought a substantial residential building in London, the Blackfriars Gatehouse, close to the theater of the same name, on March 10, 1613, he is recorded as William Shakespeare "of Stratford upon Avon in the county of Warwick, gentleman," and he named several London residents as the building's trustees. Still, he continued to participate in theatrical activity: when the new Earl of Rutland needed an allegorical design to bear as a shield, or *impresa,* at the celebration of King James's Accession Day, March 24, 1613, the earl's accountant recorded a payment of 44 shillings to Shakespeare for the device with its motto.

For the last few years of his life, Shakespeare evidently

concentrated his activities in the town of his birth. Most of the final records concern business transactions in Stratford, ending with the notation of his death on April 23, 1616, and burial in Holy Trinity Church, Stratford-upon-Avon.

THE QUESTION OF AUTHORSHIP

The history of ascribing Shakespeare's plays (the poems do not come up so often) to someone else began, as it continues, peculiarly. The earliest published claim that someone else wrote Shakespeare's plays appeared in an 1856 article by Delia Bacon in the American journal *Putnam's Monthly* – although an Englishman, Thomas Wilmot, had shared his doubts in private (even secretive) conversations with friends near the end of the eighteenth century. Bacon's was a sad personal history that ended in madness and poverty, but the year after her article, she published, with great difficulty and the bemused assistance of Nathaniel Hawthorne (then United States Consul in Liverpool, England), her *Philosophy of the Plays of Shakspere Unfolded*. This huge, ornately written, confusing farrago is almost unreadable; sometimes its intents, to say nothing of its arguments, disappear entirely beneath near-raving, ecstatic writing. Tumbled in with much supposed "philosophy" appear the claims that Francis Bacon (from whom Delia Bacon eventually claimed descent), Walter Ralegh, and several other contemporaries of Shakespeare's had written the plays. The book had little impact except as a ridiculed curiosity.

Once proposed, however, the issue gained momentum among people whose conviction was the greater in proportion to their ignorance of sixteenth- and seventeenth-century English literature, history, and society. Another American amateur, Catherine P. Ashmead Windle, made the next influential contribution to the cause when she published *Report to the British Museum* (1882), wherein she promised to open "the Cipher of Francis Bacon," though what she mostly offers, in the words of S. Schoenbaum, is "demented allegorizing." An entire new cottage industry grew from Windle's suggestion that the texts contain hidden, cryptographically discoverable ciphers – "clues" – to their authorship; and today there are not only books devoted to the putative ciphers, but also pamphlets, journals, and newsletters.

Although Baconians have led the pack of those seeking a substitute Shakespeare, in *"Shakespeare" Identified* (1920), J. Thomas Looney became the first published "Oxfordian" when he proposed Edward de Vere, seventeenth earl of Oxford, as the secret author of Shakespeare's plays. Also for Oxford and his "authorship" there are today dedicated societies, articles, journals, and books. Less popular candidates – Queen Elizabeth and Christopher Marlowe among them – have had adherents, but the movement seems to have divided into two main contending factions, Baconian and Oxfordian. (For further details on all the candidates for "Shakespeare," see S. Schoenbaum, *Shakespeare's Lives*, 2nd ed., 1991.)

The Baconians, the Oxfordians, and supporters of other candidates have one trait in common – they are snobs. Every pro-Bacon or pro-Oxford tract sooner or later claims that the historical William Shakespeare of Stratford-upon-Avon could not have written the plays because he could not have had the training, the university education, the experience, and indeed the imagination or background their author supposedly possessed. Only a learned genius like Bacon or an aristocrat like Oxford could have written such fine plays. (As it happens, lucky male children of the middle class had access to better education than most aristocrats in Elizabethan England – and Oxford was not particularly well educated.) Shakespeare received in the Stratford grammar school a formal education that would daunt many college graduates today; and popular rival playwrights such as the very learned Ben Jonson and George Chapman, both of whom also lacked university training, achieved great artistic success, without being taken as Bacon or Oxford.

Besides snobbery, one other quality characterizes the authorship controversy: lack of evidence. A great deal of testimony from Shakespeare's time shows that Shakespeare wrote Shakespeare's plays and that his contemporaries recognized them as distinctive and distinctly superior. (Some of that contemporary evidence is collected in E. K. Chambers, *William Shakespeare: A Study of Facts and Problems,* 2 vols., 1930.) Since that testimony comes from Shakespeare's enemies and theatrical competitors as well as from his co-workers and from the Elizabethan equivalent of literary journalists, it seems unlikely that, if any one of these sources had known he was a fraud, they would have failed to record that fact.

Books About Shakespeare's Theater

Useful scholarly studies of theatrical life in Shakespeare's day include: G. E. Bentley, *The Jacobean and Caroline Stage,* 7 vols. (1941-68), and the same author's *The Professions of Dramatist and Player in Shakespeare's Time, 1590-1642* (1986); E. K. Chambers, *The Elizabethan Stage,* 4 vols. (1923); R. A. Foakes, *Illustrations of the English Stage, 1580-1642* (1985); Andrew Gurr, *The Shakespearean Stage,* 3rd ed. (1992), and the same author's *Play-going in Shakespeare's London,* 2nd ed. (1996); Edwin Nungezer, *A Dictionary of Actors* (1929); Carol Chillington Rutter, ed., *Documents of the Rose Playhouse* (1984).

Books About Shakespeare's Life

The following books provide scholarly, documented accounts of Shakespeare's life: G. E. Bentley, *Shakespeare: A Biographical Handbook* (1961); E. K. Chambers, *William Shakespeare: A Study of Facts and Problems,* 2 vols. (1930); S. Schoenbaum, *William Shakespeare: A Compact*

Documentary Life (1977); and *Shakespeare's Lives,* 2nd ed. (1991), by the same author. Many scholarly editions of Shakespeare's complete works print brief compilations of essential dates and events. References to Shakespeare's works up to 1700 are collected in C. M. Ingleby et al., *The Shakespeare Allusion-Book,* rev. ed., 2 vols. (1932).

The Texts of Shakespeare

As FAR AS WE KNOW, only one manuscript conceivably in Shakespeare's own hand may (and even this is much disputed) exist: a few pages of a play called *Sir Thomas More,* which apparently was never performed. What we do have, as later readers, performers, scholars, students, are printed texts. The earliest of these survive in two forms: quartos and folios. Quartos (from the Latin for "four") are small books, printed on sheets of paper that were then folded in fours, to make eight double-sided pages. When these were bound together, the result was a squarish, eminently portable volume that sold for the relatively small sum of sixpence (translating in modern terms to about $5.00). In folios, on the other hand, the sheets are folded only once, in half, producing large, impressive volumes taller than they are wide. This was the format for important works of philosophy, science, theology, and literature (the major precedent for a folio Shakespeare was Ben Jonson's *Works,* 1616). The decision to print the works of a popular playwright in folio is an indication of how far up on the social scale the theatrical profession had come during Shakespeare's lifetime. The Shakespeare folio was an expensive book, selling for between fifteen and eighteen shillings, depending on the binding (in modern terms, from about $150 to $180). Twenty Shakespeare plays of the thirty-seven that survive first appeared in quarto, seventeen of which appeared during Shakespeare's lifetime; the rest of the plays are found only in folio.

The First Folio was published in 1623, seven years after Shakespeare's death, and was authorized by his fellow actors, the co-owners of the King's Men. This publication was certainly a mark of the company's enormous respect for Shakespeare; but it was also a way of turning the old plays, most of which were no longer current in the playhouse, into ready money (the folio includes only Shakespeare's plays, not his sonnets or other nondramatic verse). Whatever the motives behind the publication of the folio, the texts it preserves constitute the basis for almost all later editions of the playwright's works. The texts, however, differ from those of the earlier quartos, sometimes in minor respects but often significantly – most strikingly in the two texts of *King Lear,* but also in important ways in *Hamlet, Othello,* and *Troilus and Cressida.* (The variants are recorded in the textual notes to each play in the new Pelican series.) The differences in these texts represent, in a sense, the essence of theater: the texts of plays were initially not intended for publication. They were scripts, designed for the actors to perform – the principal life of the play at this period was in performance. And it follows that in Shakespeare's theater the playwright typically had no say either in how his play was performed or in the disposition of his text – he was an employee of the company. The authoritative figures in the theatrical enterprise were the shareholders in the company, who were for the most part the major actors. They decided what plays were to be done; they hired the playwright and often gave him an outline of the play they wanted him to write. Often, too, the play was a collaboration: the company would retain a group of writers, and parcel out the scenes among them. The resulting script was then the property of the company, and the actors would revise it as they saw fit during the course of putting it on stage. The resulting text belonged to the company. The playwright had no rights in it once he had been paid. (This system survives largely intact in the movie industry, and most of the playwrights of Shakespeare's time were as anonymous as most screenwriters are today.) The script could also, of course, continue to change as the tastes of audiences and the requirements of the actors changed. Many – perhaps most – plays were revised when they were reintroduced after any substantial absence from the repertory, or when they were performed by a company different from the one that originally commissioned the play.

Shakespeare was an exceptional figure in this world because he was not only a shareholder and actor in his company, but also its leading playwright – he was literally his own boss. He had, moreover, little interest in the publication of his plays, and even those that appeared during his lifetime with the authorization of the company show no signs of any editorial concern on the part of the author. Theater was, for Shakespeare, a fluid and supremely responsive medium – the very opposite of the great classic canonical text that has embodied his works since 1623.

The very fluidity of the original texts, however, has meant that Shakespeare has always had to be edited. Here is an example of how problematic the editorial project inevitably is, a passage from the most famous speech in *Romeo and Juliet,* Juliet's balcony soliloquy beginning "O Romeo, Romeo, wherefore art thou Romeo?" Since the eighteenth century, the standard modern text has read,

> What's Montague? It is nor hand, nor foot,
> Nor arm, nor face, nor any other part
> Belonging to a man. O be some other name!
> What's in a name? That which we call a rose
> By any other name would smell as sweet.
>   (II.2.40-44)

Editors have three early texts of this play to work from, two quarto texts and the folio. Here is how the First Quarto (1597) reads:

Whats *Mountague*? It is nor band nor foote,
Nor arme, nor face, nor any other part.
Whats in a name? That which we call a Rofe,
By any other name would fmell as fweet:

Here is the Second Quarto (1599):

Whats *Mountague*? it is nor hand nor foote,
Nor arme nor face, ô be fome other name
Belonging to a man.
Whats in a name that which we call a rofe,
By any other word would fmell as fweete,

And here is the First Folio (1623):

What's *Mountague*? it is nor hand nor foote,
Nor arme, nor face, O be fome other name
Belonging to a man.
What? in a names that which we call a Rofe,
By any other word would fmell as fweete,

There is in fact no early text that reads as our modern text does – and this is the most famous speech in the play. Instead, we have three quite different texts, all of which are clearly some version of the same speech, but none of which seems to us a final or satisfactory version. The transcendently beautiful passage in modern editions is an editorial invention: editors have succeeded in conflating and revising the three versions into something we recognize as great poetry. Is this what Shakespeare "really" wrote? Who can say? What we can say is that Shakespeare always had performance, not a book, in mind.

Books About the Shakespeare Texts

The standard study of the printing history of the First Folio is W. W. Greg, *The Shakespeare First Folio* (1955). J. K. Walton, *The Quarto Copy for the First Folio of Shakespeare*

(1971), is a useful survey of the relation of the quartos to the folio. The second edition of Charlton Hinman's *Norton Facsimile* of the First Folio (1996), with a new introduction by Peter Blayney, is indispensable. Stanley Wells and Gary Taylor, *William Shakespeare: A Textual Companion,* keyed to the Oxford text, gives a comprehensive survey of the editorial situation for all the plays and poems.

THE GENERAL EDITORS

Introduction

ONE OF THE CHIEF pleasures of reading *Titus Andronicus* is that it affords the experience of watching the young Shakespeare at work. Whether it was written very early in his career (c. 1590) or merely early (c. 1593), a question scholarship has yet to resolve, Shakespeare's first tragedy is clearly the effort of an ambitious and unpolished playwright – a supremely talented young man, to be sure, but one whose gifts were still to be developed. Its keynote is extravagance, as if the novice hoped to seize the attention of the London theatrical public by adopting and exaggerating the sensational form of revenge tragedy popularized by Thomas Kyd. Within the first five minutes of stage time, Shakespeare's title character mercilessly executes the son of his military enemy and then in a fit of rage stabs his own son. These acts of passion precipitate savage retribution against Titus and his family – murder, rape, the chopping off of hands, double decapitation – crimes that in turn lead to Titus's equally horrific revenge on his enemies. The final scene depicts a banquet where, before all the principal characters die, the Queen of the Goths eats a pie containing the minced bodies of her two sons. The bid for theatrical attention seems to have succeeded with the public: *Titus* was the first of Shakespeare's plays to appear in print.

Opinion about the play suffered a swift reversal in the seventeenth century, however. Edward Ravenscroft, who adapted it for the Restoration stage in 1687, declared it "the most incorrect and indigested piece in all [Shakespeare's] works; It seems rather a heap of rubbish than a structure." That judgment quickly hardened into critical orthodoxy, for over the next two and a half centuries the play was similarly reviled. T. S. Eliot described it as "one of the stupidest and most uninspired plays ever written," Tennessee Williams as "one of the most ridiculous." Until fairly recently Shakespeare's authorship has been repeatedly doubted, as if the creator of *As You Like It* and *King Lear* were incapable of producing something so crude. Only lately has *Titus* reclaimed a measure of popular and critical esteem. This second reversal of fortune is partly attributable to two influential stage productions: Peter Brook's at Stratford-upon-Avon in 1955, with Laurence Olivier as Titus and Vivien Leigh as Lavinia; and Deborah Warner's 1987 staging for the Royal Shakespeare Company in the Swan Theatre, also at Stratford, with Brian Cox as Titus and Estelle Kohler as Tamora. Tradition had declared *Titus* absurd, but theatergoers found themselves engaged and emotionally stirred. The Polish critic Jan Kott summarized this conflict in his response to the Brook production: "I have recently reread it, and found it ridiculous. I have seen it on the stage, and found it a moving experience. Why?"

Why indeed? Kott's antithetical reactions expose a truth that has obtained for the past four centuries, that the play's harshest detractors have been those who have not seen it well performed, or even performed at all. In our own time, as in Shakespeare's, theatrical realization of the text has generated comment, respect, and fascination. In addition to the theatrical explanation, there are cultural and critical reasons for renewed attention to *Titus*. Recent Anglo-American culture, familiar as it is with violence in art (slasher films) and life (two world wars), has accustomed audiences to the kind of brutality that *Titus* exploits. Closer acquaintance with the play has revealed its links to such masterpieces as *Hamlet* and *King Lear* and thus has increased respect for it. And it has to be said that modern Bardolatry – reverence for all things Shakespearean – may have led us to look more sympathetically on a manifestly youthful and uneven effort. No one ranks

Titus among the greatest of its creator's achievements, but it is indisputably his work, and in many respects typical. To read it with a theatrical imagination is to observe the young Shakespeare attempting to establish himself as a tragic writer and tentatively addressing many of the human problems that would occupy him for the remainder of his theatrical career.

The novice's wish to be noticed declares itself in his decision to write a revenge tragedy. The standard for this dramatic mode was Thomas Kyd's *The Spanish Tragedy* (c. 1587), probably the most famous and popular English play before *Hamlet:* in formal terms *Titus* is an imitation of Kyd's thriller. The most celebrated playwright of the moment was Kyd's friend and sometime roommate, Christopher Marlowe, whose charismatic heroes were speaking a new and eloquent verse from the stage of the Rose theater at about the time William Shakespeare arrived in London from the provinces. Uncertainty about when *Titus* was composed requires caution in thinking about contemporary influences and its author's own artistic maturity. Some scholars place it around 1590-92, which would make it one of Shakespeare's earliest plays. Alternatively, he may have written it expressly for the recorded performances in January 1594 that resulted in its publication, working on it at the end of 1593 when the theaters were about to reopen following nearly two years of plague. (This staging may have been a revival, however, a later production of a popular text – now possibly revised – originally written at the beginning of the decade.) In 1590 Shakespeare would have known the two parts of *Tamburlaine* as well as the crucial Marlovian pre-text, *The Jew of Malta;* by the later date he would have been familiar with all Marlowe's dramas. Regardless of its date, *Titus* was still something of an apprentice play, for even if Shakespeare had already produced seven or eight plays before undertaking it, the effort to create what Sidney called "high and excellent tragedy" would have been a new challenge.

Passion, murder, vengeance, conspiracy, gore – these delights appear not only in the revenge plays of Marlowe and Kyd but also in other contemporary tragedies and historical dramas. What distinguishes *The Spanish Tragedy* and *The Jew of Malta* is a kind of theatrical exuberance, a pleasure in excess, and it is this audacity that Shakespeare seems to have deliberately mimicked in *Titus*. In *The Spanish Tragedy* Kyd terrorizes his audience with the effects of unaccountable evil: a ghost's demand for revenge initiates the action, in which a jealous suitor stabs and hangs his rival in a garden; Hieronimo, the father of the victim, begins a quest for vengeance; the consequences include madness, the suicide of his wife, and a bloody final scene in which Hieronimo, to avoid speaking, bites out his own tongue and spits it across the stage before stabbing one of his enemies and himself with a penknife. Thus *The Spanish Tragedy* works more or less like the modern horror film, simultaneously frightening and titillating the protected viewer with the illusion of violent action. *The Jew of Malta,* which T. S. Eliot described as "a savage farce," displays its atrocities with similar zest: "I walk abroad a' nights / And kill sick people groaning under walls: / Sometimes I go about and poison wells." In Hieronimo, Kyd created a passionate father driven to insanity by the injustice of the world, and Shakespeare borrowed details of that portrait in representing the experience of his suffering patriarch. In Barabas, the Jewish outsider who is the villain-hero of *The Jew of Malta,* Marlowe adapted the popular figure of the Machiavel, the Italian villain loosely deriving from the political writings of Niccolò Machiavelli. He thus supplied an immediate model for Shakespeare's Aaron, the wicked Moor who becomes the principal agent of Titus's misery. In short, Kyd spotlights the victim, Marlowe the villain, and Shakespeare invents a vivid example of each. There are other affinities between these plays and *Titus:* the showmanship with which Hieronimo and Barabas pursue their final revenge seems especially to have appealed to the young playwright. Hieronimo, for example, concocts a theatrical piece in which fictional violence turns out to be actual – he murders his son's murderers in a play – and the theater audience, knowing the trick in advance, relishes the ignorance of the stage spectators. But all these resemblances matter less than Shakespeare's adopting his predecessors' complex attitude toward their material. Thanks mainly to their example and their success, he developed an extraordinary mixture of horror and humor, an interplay of engagement and detachment that permits the spectator to take pleasure in a fictional story of cruelty and suffering.

In planning his first tragedy Shakespeare also looked beyond the local scene. We might say that for *Titus,* rather than adapt an ancient tragedy, he classicized the contemporary revenge play. Considering the reproach Shakespeare was later to suffer at the hands of Ben Jonson (and other critics over the next four centuries) for his reputed "small Latin," this represents a significant maneuver. Kyd and Marlowe, products of a university system as Shakespeare was not, were almost certainly more conversant than he with classical literature. Nevertheless, he set out to write a Roman play, joining the conventions of Elizabethan revenge tragedy with those of Latin tragedy, giving the action an ancient setting, and coloring the narrative with references to pertinent episodes from Ovid, Virgil, and other classical authors. *Titus* may be regarded not only as an Elizabethan revenge play but also as a Senecan tragedy, a mode in which the fearless hero brutally exacts revenge upon equally vicious opponents. For one of his first comedies, *The Comedy of Errors,* Shakespeare went to Plautus, one of the two acknowledged masters of Roman comedy, and in borrowing from Seneca – the cannibalism at the end of *Thyestes,* for instance – he exhibited the same respect for classical example. But his dependence upon the Romans is not limited to the playwrights. In particular the story of Philomel and Tereus, from Ovid's

Metamorphoses, probably Shakespeare's favorite book, serves as a constant referent for the action in *Titus,* as do other classical tales and persons: Virginius's daughter, killed by her father to cancel the shame of rape; the chaste Lucrece, about whose rape Shakespeare had recently completed a narrative poem; and, of course, Aeneas, founder of the empire, and his bride, Lavinia. The proportions of influence and originality are difficult to calculate here because Kyd and Marlowe had themselves appropriated many of the Senecan conventions, so it is unclear whether Shakespeare was imitating Seneca or Seneca's imitators. But it is safe to say that classical legacy contributes much to making his first tragedy what it is.

Modern scholarship has agreed to think of *Titus Andronicus* as Shakespeare's first tragedy, but in accepting such a designation we need to recognize the anachronism and ambiguity of the phrase. To the Elizabethan mind the noun "tragedy" was much more fluid than modern usage has made it, describing any dramatic (or even narrative) work that depicted a fall from high place and ended in death or sorrow. By this measure some of Shakespeare's early history plays qualify as tragedies and were so considered by their original audiences and readers: the early printed version of *Henry VI, Part 3* is advertised on the title page as *The True Tragedy of Richard, Duke of York.* The process was also reversible, as we know from the 1608 Quarto of one of Shakespeare's most celebrated tragedies, *The History of King Lear.* Our own more rigid system of classification began with the 1623 First Folio, which groups together as "Histories" all his dramas about the English monarchy, regardless of their endings.

Although the decision of the folio editors accounts for our thinking of *Titus* as Shakespeare's first tragedy, we may fairly suppose that the dramatist thought of himself as working in a form new to him. Its status as a first effort helps to account for the critical condescension it has suffered, an attitude reinforced by its debts to the popular theater of the day: flagrant violence, relatively undeveloped characterization, and a rough-and-ready verse style. It is like the other tragedies, but perhaps not enough like them. Its horrific actions seem superficial compared to those of *Hamlet*. The tragic figure lacks the interiority characteristic of, say, Macbeth. Not only does Titus deliver no great soliloquies, he doesn't seem to grow as a result of his afflictions, much less to triumph spiritually. One critical response to disappointment was to doubt Shakespeare's authorship of *Titus,* and the discovery of the only surviving copy of the First Quarto (in 1904) seemed to confirm such suspicions, for it identifies no author either on the title page or elsewhere. An alternative theory, developed from an oblique hint dropped in the middle of the seventeenth century, held that Shakespeare had at most touched up the labors of an inferior colleague. The quarto text contains evidence of false starts: for example, the killing of Alarbus seems to have been added late, since it contradicts some earlier lines implying that the sacrifice has already been performed. Still, even after twentieth-century scholarship persuasively established Shakespeare's authorship, critics felt obliged to apologize for the sensationalism, the vulgarity, the immaturity of *Titus*. Most offensive to many commentators were the very theatrical effects that made the play a success at the Rose and that still ensure its power on the stage – Titus's stabbing his own son, the rape and mutilation of Lavinia, the glee with which Titus (in his chef's getup) serves the human pastry to Tamora and murders his own daughter. The spectacle was too much for later sensibilities, particularly for the decorum of the nineteenth-century theater, and those Victorian reservations remain influential. To many *Titus* is still hopelessly crude; it is an embarrassment to its author; it offers little more than, as Wagner said about a rival's operas, "effects without causes."

It is pointless to deny that *Titus* is less controlled, perhaps less profound, certainly less polished than the tragedies its creator would go on to write. Possibly he had not yet developed a thoroughgoing tragic vision of human experience, the complex understanding of inescapable evil and human vulnerability informing such plays as *Othello* and *Macbeth*. It may be that Shakespeare wrote the play not to express deeply held convictions about the iniquities of the world or to probe the nature of tragic passion, but simply to try his hand at tragedy, to give his company a vehicle for attracting customers to a serious drama. In other words, its origin seems somehow external. But its theatrical effects can still produce a powerful impact upon audiences in the theater, as great productions unfailingly demonstrate, and to approach the text sympathetically – to read it, in other words, historically – is to sense that its bloody spectacle is a manifestation of tragic perceptions that Shakespeare would soon explore more completely and persuasively.

Mature Shakespearean tragedy recognizes and laments the self-destructive impulse in virtually all human interaction, and the career of Titus conforms to the pattern. According to this paradigm, the hero is inevitably fatal to himself, virtue necessarily bound up with evil. All the tragedies insist upon the protagonist's responsibility for his own downfall – his own hand in his tragedy, we might say – and Shakespeare seems to have literalized this theme in Act Three of *Titus*, when the grieving father agrees to chop off his own hand and send it to the emperor as ransom for his sons. The tragic figure thus commits himself to the course of self-destruction and naively enlists the help of evil forces, here also literalized, in the person of Aaron: "Lend me thy hand, and I will give thee mine" (III.1.187). This moment epitomizes the moral structure of the tragedy, creating an unforgettable image of self-annihilation. Almost as soon as the action begins, savagery breaks out, most obviously in Titus's murder of his son Mutius for opposing his will, and it quickly escalates with the murder of Bassianus, the rape of Lavinia, and the decapitation of Titus's sons. These atrocities follow directly from Titus's own passionate act, but the horrific actions for which the play is notorious are not peculiar to Titus and his immediate family. Rape, self-mutilation, and cannibalism represent the logical extension of an atrocious code of honor on which Rome is founded and of which Titus is the principal guarantor.

Titus's honorific name is Pius, an appellation identified in the Renaissance with Aeneas: an adjectival form of the Roman ideal *pietas,* it means not only "religious" but also "honorable" and "patriotic." Shakespeare's treatment of these virtues discloses that they are more ambiguous than they at first appear. Titus's first patriotic act is human sacrifice, the murder of Alarbus despite the pleas of his captive mother, and in doing so he illegitimately presumes upon divine authority ("Wilt thou draw near the nature of the gods?"). As her son is carried off to torture and execution, Tamora condemns her captors' "cruel irreligious piety," and in that phrase Shakespeare identifies the contradiction that informs Roman military ritual. "Honor" in Rome entails loyalty to a brutal code of retribution. Titus has already lost twenty-one sons in the wars against Rome's enemies; in sustaining the code of honor he murders one of his four remaining sons; and the further deaths of Quintus and Martius and the mutilation of Lavinia are shown to be consequences of his devotion to this code, since his sacrifice of Alarbus sets into motion the revenge of Tamora against Titus and his family. In theory, Titus's commitment to Rome is laudable; in practice it is "cruel" and "irreligious." In representing the conflict between ideal and reality, *Titus* offers intimations of the tragic paradox that Shakespeare will explore more thoroughly in the later tragedies: the perils of Hamlet's supreme intelligence, for example, or the disastrous end of Othello's passion. And even in this early effort the pattern of self-ruin is projected into several realms of human endeavor – the familial, the political, the sexual. Lucius's invasion of Rome with an army of Goths, like the vengeance of Coriolanus explicitly mentioned as a model, offers a telling instance of this ironic design.

Stimulated by the conventions of revenge tragedy and responding to contemporary taste for pattern and analogy, Shakespeare multiplies the structural parallels and other forms of repetition in *Titus*. The theme of retribution lends itself to such mirroring. Tamora takes revenge for the execution of her son by assailing Titus's offspring; he replicates her crime by murdering her two remaining sons. No less than four pairs of brothers populate the play. Saturninus and Bassianus open the first act disputing over the throne and marital possession of Lavinia; Chiron and Demetrius begin the second act quarreling over sexual possession of Lavinia; Quintus and Martius are decapitated in Act Three; and Marcus and Titus console each other throughout. A coffin is brought onstage in Act One for the burial of Titus's sons slain in the war against Tamora and the Goths; another appears in Act Five as Titus bakes a "coffin," or pie-crust, for the flesh of Tamora's sons. The exceptional allusiveness of the text, in which historical episodes and legends are summoned as precedents for the stage action, represents the characters' desire to identify the continuities of experience. Lavinia uses an actual copy of Ovid's Philomel story to articulate the details of the rape, and Titus cites the story of Virginius and his violated daughter as "A pattern, precedent, and lively warrant / For me, most wretched, to perform the like" (V.3.44-45). This passion for replication serves the characters as a defense against confusion; it serves Shakespeare as a means of ordering experience into an artistic object of admirable shape. It also reveals his joy – and that of his audience – in the pleasures of design.

This fondness for pattern expresses itself conspicuously in his devotion to contrariety. If drama is conflict, then *Titus* is exceedingly dramatic, with opposition governing every facet of the work. The staging moves up and down from main stage to gallery to pit as the action rises and falls. The thematic structure explores a range of antitheses (Roman and Goth, civilization and barbarism, masculine and feminine). Even at the level of the line, words contest each other oxymoronically ("irreligious piety"). Obviously Shakespeare pits single characters and groups against each other, but what points the way to maturity is his tendency to combine opposites within a single figure. Emotionally, of course, Titus is the touchstone for such contradiction, and Tamora plays both grieving mother and pitiless avenger, protective wife and eager adulteress. The portrait of Aaron, however, offers the most striking evocation of contempt and sympathy.

As a Moor (or blackamoor), Aaron probably would have served the Elizabethan audience as a magnet for revulsion. Much is made of his race, which the Romans regard Platonically, as if dark skin signified an evil soul. He would seem to stand as the extreme case of the cultural Other, a barbarian inimical to the civilized empire. But Shakespeare, even in this early phase, disallows such easy oppositions. The villain's name would have had positive, biblical associations for Elizabethan audiences: Aaron, the brother of Moses, helped to lead the chosen people out of Egypt and served as the first priest of the children of Israel. And Shakespeare subverts the conventional sense of barbarism by showing the Romans, before Aaron ever speaks, to be as potentially uncivilized as the Goths. Similarly, Aaron's talents as a wisecracker confound expectation. The glee with which he snookers Titus into giving up his hand, for example, complicates an audience's emotional reaction to one of the most ghastly events in the play. Humor lightens his malevolence for a time, but the jokes rapidly fade in light of his monstrous behavior. This includes, but is not limited to, adultery, forgery, planting evidence, incitement to rape, slander leading to decapitation of the innocent, dismemberment, promise-breaking, and outright murder. Late in the play Shakespeare introduces yet another turn, in the person of Aaron's infant son, over whom the killer smiles and coos. Moments later, he viciously stabs the child's nurse while mocking her dying cries. Such emotional oscillation in our response to character is part of Shakespeare's larger design in *Titus*. It is also, of course, the key to the complex power of the great tragedies.

Rhetorical patterns are most easily apprehended by the ear, and *Titus* emphatically announces the young Shakespeare's prodigious gift for language. The sound of the poetry – virtually all the play is written in verse, with only one brief episode in prose – is typical of his early style. The speakers deliver a thumpingly regular iambic pentameter. Most lines are free of the metrical variations such as inverted feet or eleven-syllable lines that would later enter the poet's repertoire. Such uniformity is underscored, moreover, by yet another pattern, congruence between the semantic and the poetic units. In other words, the lines tend to be endstopped because the end of the sentence or clause usually coincides with the end of the line rather than pushing over into the next. The opening pair of lines illustrates his normal practice at this period: "Noble patricians, patrons of my right, / Defend the justice of my cause with arms" (I.1.1-2). The regularity of these stops throughout *Titus* implies that the apprentice playwright approached the task of poetic composition by thinking in ten-syllable units. As he becomes more practiced at the writing of verse he will vary this pattern as well, enjambing lines and introducing frequent midline stops. Such poetic uniformity does not permit the kind of subtlety audible in the familiar speeches of a Hamlet or Lear, where nuance derives from aural strategies such as rhythmic variety, hesitation, the creation of momentum, or shifts in tempo. But it does offer the virtues of directness and rhythmic inevitability.

The verse, in other words, provides a sonic simulacrum

of the represented action – straightforward, blunt, and forceful. Over the course of the entire play, some twenty-five hundred lines, most of them endstopped, the listener's ear becomes accustomed to a pattern of congruity and equivalence. Such lineal consistency also characterizes most of the poetry in the early comedies and histories, and the arrangement of poetic language into lines of equivalent length conveys sensually the stark oppositions on which the action is based, creating, in the words of G. R. Hibbard, a "pattern of total opposition and balanced confrontation." In *Titus,* such verbal patterning magnifies the multiple contrarieties: Saturninus versus Bassianus in the opening scene, the contention of the opposed couples (Saturninus and Tamora, Bassianus and Lavinia), Demetrius and Chiron squabbling over Lavinia, Demetrius and Chiron versus Quintus and Martius, Tamora versus Titus, Romans versus Goths. The distinctive aural imprint is especially noticeable when *Titus* is compared to *Romeo and Juliet,* Shakespeare's second tragedy, written perhaps only a year or so later. The love story invites lyricism and a greater range of emotion. In the Roman tragedy, however, the brutality of the narrative accounts for emphatic sounds and lack of variety.

Titus is not unpoetic. The difficulty is that its poetic properties do not function in a conventionally lyrical fashion. The most famously "poetic" speech, Marcus's Ovidian meditation on the maimed Lavinia, is so notoriously incongruous with its bloody context that most directors either fiercely abbreviate or even eliminate it. Those passages that would seem to be rhapsodic usually work ironically, such as Tamora's praise of the forest, which exposes the speaker's adulterous sensuality. Many lines glitter with verbal imagery, particularly in the form of simile and metaphor, but (not surprisingly, given the nature of the action) the discursive field is mostly confined to the animal kingdom: wasps, flies, whelps, owls and ravens, snakes, adders, urchins (hedgehogs), hellhounds, lions and lionesses, curs, tigers, pigs, panthers, boars, stags and does, swans, toads, slaughtered lambs, and an army of goats ("Goth" and "goat" were homonyms, as indicated by Touchstone's pun in *As You Like It*). Descriptive images of landscape are often sexualized, most obviously in the vaginal connotations of the deadly pit at the center of the dark forest: it is transformed poetically into an "unhallowed and blood-stained hole," a "loathsome pit," a "subtle hole," "this abhorred pit," "the swallowing womb," a "detested, dark, blood-drinking pit."

The wordplay is as extravagant as the imagery, as emphatic as the rhythms:

> NURSE
>   O, tell me, did you see Aaron the Moor?
> AARON
>   Well, more or less, or ne'er a whit at all.
> (IV.2.52-53)

Beginning with the pun on "Moor" and continuing with a play on "whit" and "white," Aaron's retort reveals the gap between early modern taste and our own view of linguistic play. Modern contempt for such verbal turns, conditioned by utilitarian views of language that originated in the Enlightenment and solidified in the nineteenth century, may keep us from recognizing that Shakespeare's audience took apparently limitless pleasure in the plasticity of verbal signs. The field of play was considerably wider than our own, first because pronunciation was more flexible than it has since become, and second because the English language was in a period of expansion, with words regularly being added, especially from Latin roots. The prominence of homonymic puns in early modern writing indicates that Elizabethan playgoers received the spoken word with greater sensitivity to the medium than we normally enjoy. Dramatists customarily called attention to the surface of the language, manipulating the various meanings of words to satisfy contemporary taste for rhetorical display and poetic ornament. Puns were made to perform specific tasks as well: to particularize a speaker, especially to suggest mental or verbal ingenuity; to summon up thematically relevant meanings concealed in a word or phrase; to reveal the delightful multiplicity of language; to reveal the dangerous multiplicity of language; to advertise and celebrate the writer's powers of verbal ingenuity.

The puns in *Titus,* like the violence, are so abundant and conspicuous that they must be taken as part of Shakespeare's audacious bid for professional notice. The exchange between the Nurse and Aaron quoted above occurs in a scene that abounds with witty turns: on "issue" (outcome and offspring), on "rest" (remain and repose), on "delivered" (sent, set free, given birth), on "Horace" (Whore-ass), and, most strikingly, on "do" and "undo":

> DEMETRIUS
> Villain, what hast thou done?
> AARON
> That which thou canst not undo.
> CHIRON
> Thou hast undone our mother.
> AARON
> Villain, I have done thy mother.
> (IV.2.73-76)

Aaron's scoffing implies a kind of verbal energy that Shakespeare often confers upon his villains, notably Richard III and Iago. As with those psychopaths, his verbal facility connotes an imaginative amorality that extends to the manipulation of persons and events. In other words, Aaron's aggressive way with words helps the audience to place him in the moral landscape as ingenious, dangerous, and amusing. When, for example, he taunts his captors with the narrative of his crimes, his language seems to explode with double and triple meanings.

AARON
   They cut thy sister's tongue, and ravished her,
   And cut her hands, and *trimmed* her as thou *sawest*.
LUCIUS
   O detestable villain! call'st thou that trimming?
AARON
   Why, she was washed and cut and *trimmed*, and 'twas
   Trim sport for them which had the doing of it.
                                   (V.1.92–96, my italics)

Changes in the verb "trim" have robbed this passage of some of its brutality: "to trim" meant not only to cut, but also to tidy, to put in good order, to decorate. According to Aaron, rape has improved Lavinia. Lucius recoils at the initial joke, which Aaron then augments, drawing upon the sense of "trim" as "beautiful" or "fine."

Homonymic extravagance is not confined to the wicked, however. Almost everyone indulges in it, implying that the most determined punster is Shakespeare himself and that his attachment to verbal ambiguity is to some degree a response to cultural expectation. The ambiguity also functions instrumentally, as we might expect. The frequent play on "Goths / goats" illustrates the thematic value of double meanings, contributing to the imagistic menagerie ("a band of warlike goats / Goths") and reinforcing the opposition – an unstable one, to be sure – between civilization and barbarism, Romans and Goths, humans and goats.

The most unsettling puns are delivered by Titus himself, and the word that he reiterates most obsessively is "hands." When Marcus brings the raped and mutilated Lavinia to Titus, the beleaguered old man reacts first with what we would consider a lame joke: "Speak, Lavinia, what accursèd hand / Hath made thee handless in thy father's sight?" (III.1.66-67). Scarcely a hundred lines later, Titus has yielded up his own hand. When Marcus seeks to protect Lavinia from self-inflicted injury – "teach her not thus to lay / Such violent hands upon her tender life" (III.2.21-22) – Titus objects to his brother's figurative usage, literalizing the phrase ("lay hands upon") in a passage that critics have usually found embarrassing.

> What violent hands can she lay on her life?
> Ah, wherefore dost thou urge the name of
>   hands. . . .
> O, handle not the theme, to talk of hands,
> Lest we remember still that we have none.
>   (III.2.25-30)

The quibble on "handle" is not an aberration but typical in its obviousness and indecorum. Titus plays with words in a way that seems indecent or grotesque. His equivocation is not, however, essentially different from that of other tragic figures who pun at apparently inappropriate times: as it sometimes does in *King Lear,* for example, the slippery language here indicates a kind of obsessive distraction, as if only a madman could jest about such painful occurrences. But still the frequency is exceptional. The noun "hand" is used (in its singular and plural forms) almost eighty times in *Titus,* more than in any other play, and such worrying of the same word represents a kind of verbal gesticulation on the part of the dramatist.

The hand here affords Shakespeare a symbol of agency. Titus's fame rests on his military skill ("which of your hands hath not defended Rome?"); his "warlike hand" is an emblem of his achievement ("LAVINIA: O, bless me here with thy victorious hand"); Titus "with his own hand did slay his youngest son"; the opening quarrel between Saturninus and Bassianus concerns the right to the imperial scepter (held in the hand); the succeeding dispute over Lavinia concerns her hand in marriage, over which the patriarchal Titus exercises authority; Saturninus resents having "begged the empire at [Titus's] hands." Elsewhere in the play the puns on "arms," along with "army" and the "armory" where young Lucius is outfitted, do similar work, standing metonymically for human strength and its loss. The concentrated equivocation in the two scenes that constitute Act Three focuses the audience's gaze on the play's central images of powerlessness, Lavinia's bleeding stumps, and Titus's own severed limb. And the double entendre on "handle," perhaps the most outrageous of the many puns having to do with dismemberment, punctuates the dramatist's concern with the fundamental problems of cruelty, suffering, and self-destruction. Even "government," the term that comprises the multiple conflicts of *Titus*, comes from a Greek word meaning "to steer." The issue here is control.

Revenge tragedy, of course, takes upon itself to dramatize the lack of control that humans feel in a chaotic world. Kyd's Hieronimo suffers so intensely because – despite his office as Chief Justice of Spain – he cannot attain a legal remedy for the murder of his son. For Titus, the rape and butchering of Lavinia, and the following decapitation of Quintus and Martius, mark the stages of his decline; the surrender of his own hand provides an additional emblem for his reduced authority. There are other kinds of power than the political, however. As Titus loses political and judicial control, he begins, like the heroes of other revenge tragedies, to gain rhetorical and theatrical command. The term "vengeance" comes from the Latin *vindicare*, a combination of *vim*, or power, with *dicere*, to speak. Titus's rhetorical strength manifests itself in the form of great poetic laments ("For now I stand as one upon a rock"), mad hilarity in the face of unspeakable pain ("Ha, ha, ha"), and the volley of outrageous quibbles. Significantly, Titus seeks his ultimate revenge in a theatrical performance, wearing a chef's costume "to be sure to have all well" and cooking up the scheme to destroy Tamora and Saturninus. His culinary outfit, like the banquet he hosts, is the visual equivalent of the pun, a witty text with a murderous subtext that permits the victim to regain a measure of lost authority.

As a cultural object, *Titus Andronicus* itself bears a double meaning. It is both a horror show and a work by Shakespeare, and it is this doubleness that makes the play especially meaningful, both as a work of theater and as an earnest of the young playwright's future achievements. In the baldness of its wordplay and the grotesque instability of many of its stage images, poised as they are between comedy and pathos, *Titus* can seem shocking, crude, even, as its critical history suggests, inept. And yet this mixture of effects is what gives the play its distinctive flavor. Deborah Warner, directing the 1987 Royal Shakespeare Company production, exaggerated the tonal incongruities rather than conceal them. She forestalled inappropriate laughter in the audience by initiating it from the stage, encouraging Brian Cox, her Titus, to signal his awareness of the grisly humor lurking in his tragic experience. As his servants carried the banquet table onto the stage in Act Five, they whistled the dwarves' jaunty melody ("Whistle While You Work") from Disney's *Snow White.*

Shakespeare's most sophisticated attempt at mingling sensations occurs immediately after the rape: *"Enter the Empress' sons [Demetrius and Chiron], with Lavinia, her hands cut off, and her tongue cut out, and ravished."* The audience is confronted by Lavinia's violated body, the rapists' disgusting jokes about her maiming, and, immediately thereafter, her uncle's poetic excursus on her misery: "Alas, a crimson river of warm blood, / Like to a bubbling fountain stirred with wind, / Doth rise and fall between thy rosèd lips" (II.4.22-24). Lavinia becomes an object of pity and terror: into that image Shakespeare has concentrated the play's abiding concern with human affliction, debilitation, lack of agency, the inadequacy of speech, the pathos of human impotence. This moment may stand for each of the puzzling and meaningful episodes in the play, from the killing of Mutius to the cannibalistic banquet. Each entails a kind of imaginative exercise, demanding that the audience consider human action from multiple points of view. Laughter, pathos, revulsion, poetry all conspire to enlarge our awareness of the implications of human action. And it is this multiplicity that ultimately accounts for an audience's profoundly divided response to Falstaff, Macbeth, and Cleopatra.

I began with the emergence of *Titus* from the contemporary theatrical milieu, and I shall end with its emergence from the theater of Elizabethan politics. The conflicts of the plot arise initially from competition for the imperial throne, Shakespeare apparently having obscured deliberately the basis for succession in Titus's Rome. When the play was new, Elizabeth I was about sixty years old, childless, and adamant in refusing to designate an heir. So deep were the religious divisions among Puritans, middle-of-the-road Protestants, and would-be Catholics, and so virulent were the feelings of each faction, that the possibility of civil war at the queen's death seemed real and terrifying. Fears of Spanish invasion remained in the air despite the recent defeat of the Armada. And the future was not the only source of alarm: many in the 1590s privately deplored Elizabeth's absolutism, and republican sentiments were held by a group of thinkers that Shakespeare probably knew personally. *Titus* is a thriller, but it is also political drama, a theatrical representation of the dangers of tyranny, and as such it speaks to issues with which many a Londoner would have been constantly occupied.

It is probably fair to say also that the violence of *Titus* is partly a cultural product. English political life in the last decades of the sixteenth century was treacherous and potentially fatal, a shadowy realm of religious intrigue, talk of treason, assassination attempts, and dirty tricks performed by the queen's secret police. The brutality of the age is attested by the career of a Protestant zealot named John Stubbs. In 1579, as Elizabeth considered marriage to the French Duke of Alençon, Stubbs composed a pamphlet ferociously opposing the match on the grounds of the suitor's Catholicism. The crown retaliated with a trial and with one of its most effective methods of social control, the spectacle of public punishment: Stubbs and his publisher were sentenced to have their right hands cut off and then to be imprisoned. On the scaffold, concluding a polemical defense of his patriotism, Stubbs requested the assembly's blessing in a shocking pun: "Pray for me now my calamity is at hand." At that point the ax fell, and Stubbs fainted. The young Shakespeare may have heightened and arranged the pain and violence represented in *Titus,* but he did not entirely invent it. While many of his contemporaries proudly looked to ancient Rome as a paradigm for English imperial ambition, Shakespeare apparently looked also to contemporary England as a pattern for his Roman drama.

RUSS MCDONALD
University of North Carolina at Greensboro

Note on the Text

TITUS ANDRONICUS WAS FIRST published in quarto in 1594, the first of Shakespeare's plays to appear in print. The quarto text (Q1), despite some obvious errors and problematic punctuation, is on the whole superior to later printings and thus serves as copy text for the present edition. Certain features in Q1, such as sketchy stage directions (e.g., I.1.72, *enter . . . others as many as can be*) and inconsistent speech prefixes (e.g., *Saturninus* is also identified as *King* and *Emperor*) suggest that it derives from an authorial or scribal manuscript produced relatively early in the collaborative process, not from a polished theatrical script.

The Second Quarto was printed in 1600 from a damaged copy of the 1594 text. As a result, the printer apparently tried to reconstruct lines that were illegible in his source copy: six passages near the end of the play, including the last four lines of Q2 (relegated to a footnote in the present edition), appear to be his – or someone's – invention. Although the punctuation in Q2 was improved and a number of mistakes corrected, many new errors crept into the text. The Third Quarto, printed from the Second, introduces still more errors and a few corrections.

The folio text (F1) reproduces the errors of Q3, from which it was printed, but it provides many additional stage directions and, invaluably, prints a full scene (III.2) not found in any of the quartos. The editors of the folio apparently supplemented their copy text (Q3) with a manuscript of the additional scene; there is no reason to doubt its authenticity, and so the present edition departs from Q1 in printing the scene from F1.

Speech prefixes have been normalized and punctuation

and spelling modernized. The act divisions derive from F1, scene divisions from editorial tradition.

What follows is a list of the readings in this edition that differ significantly from the text of Q1. Minor corrections unrelated to meaning are not noted. The adopted reading is given in italics, followed by the rejected Q1 reading in roman. Parentheses following the italic reading indicate the source of the correction: e.g., (Q2); the absence of parentheses means that the reading is an emendation suggested by scholars or earlier editors.

I.1 36 *the Andronici* that Andronicy   58 **s.d.** *Exeunt* Exit   74 *her* (F4) his   92 *bretheren* (Q3) brethren   101 *manes* (F3) manus   132 **s.d.** *Exeunt* Exit   229 *Titan's* (Q2) Tytus   245 *Pantheon* (F2) Pathan   267 *chance* (Q2) change   283 *cuique* (F2) cuiqum   319 *Phoebe* (F2) Thebe   353 *hundred* hundreth   360 *bretheren* (Q3) brethren   **s.d.** *speak* speakes   367 *struck* stroke   393 **s.d.** *Exeunt* Exit   401 *Yes . . . remunerate* (F; omitted in Qq)   477–79 *We do . . . our own* (assigned as in F; given to Tamora in Qq)

II.1 93 *struck* stroke   110 *than* this

II.2 1 *morn* (Q3) Moone

II.3 13 *snake* (Q3) snakes   69 *try experiments* (Q2) trie thy experimens   72 *swart* swartie   85 *note* notice   110 *Lascivious* (Q3) Lauicious   118 *Ay,* I   132 *outlive, us* out live us   144 *suck'dst* suck'st   160 *ears* (Q3) yeares   198 *What,* (F4) What   210 *unhallowed* (F) unhollow   222 *berayed* bereaud   231 *Pyramus* (Q2) Priamus   236 *Cocytus'* (F2) Ocitus   286 *What,* What   291 *fault* faults   296 *father's* fathers

II.4 27 *him* them   30 *three* their   38 *Philomel* Philomela

III.1 9 *are* (F2) is   17 *urns* ruines   34 *or* (Q2; omitted in Q1)   146 *with his* (F4) with her   169 *casque* castle   225 *blow* (F2) flow   281 *employed [. . .]* imployde in these Armes

III.2 (this scene appears only in F)   39 *complainer* complainet   52 *thy* (omitted in F)   53 *fly* Flys   54 *thee,* (F3) the   55 *are* (omitted in F)   72 *myself* my selfes

IV.1 10 MARCUS (speech prefix omitted in Q)   50 *quotes* (Q2) coats   78 TITUS (Q3, F; speech prefix omitted in Q)   88 *hope* (Q2) hop [or: I op]   91 *sware* (F3) sweare

IV.2 95 *Alcides* (Q2) Alciades   179 *fat* feede

IV.3 57 *Saturn," Caius* Saturnine, to Caius   78 *News . . . come* (assigned to Clown in Q)   81 *Who* Ho

IV.4 5 *know, as know* know   49 *By' lady* be Lady   62 **s.d.** *Nuntius* (Q2) Nutius   94 *feed* (Q3) seed   99 *ears* (F) yeares

V.1 16 *avenged* (Q3) aduengde   53 *Get . . . ladder* (assigned to Aaron in Q)   133 *haystacks* haystalks

V.2 18 *it action* (F) that accord **49** *globe* globes **52** *murderers* murder; *caves* (F2) cares **56** *Hyperion's* (F2) Epeons **61** *Are they* (F2) Are them
V.3 125 *cause* (F4) course **141** ALL (assigned to Marcus in Q) **144** *adjudged* (Q3) adiudge **146** ALL (assigned to Marcus in Q) **154** *blood-stained* (F3) blood slaine **163** *Sung* (Q2) Song **172** BOY Puer

Titus Andronicus

[NAMES OF THE ACTORS

SATURNINUS, *son of the late Emperor of Rome, later declared Emperor*

BASSIANUS, *brother of Saturninus; in love with Lavinia*

TITUS ANDRONICUS, *a noble Roman, general against the Goths*

MARCUS ANDRONICUS, *tribune of the people, brother of Titus*

LUCIUS
QUINTUS } *sons of Titus Andronicus*
MARTIUS
MUTIUS

YOUNG LUCIUS, *a boy, son of Lucius*

PUBLIUS, *son of Marcus Andronicus*

SEMPRONIUS
CAIUS } *kinsmen of Titus Andronicus*
VALENTINE

AEMILIUS, *a noble Roman*

ALARBUS
DEMETRIUS } *sons of Tamora*
CHIRON

AARON, *a Moor, lover of Tamora*

A CAPTAIN

A MESSENGER

A CLOWN

TAMORA, *Queen of the Goths*

LAVINIA, *daughter of Titus Andronicus*

A NURSE, AND A BLACK CHILD

ROMANS AND GOTHS, SENATORS, TRIBUNES, OFFICERS, SOLDIERS, ATTENDANTS

SCENE: *Rome and the surrounding countryside*]

*

Titus Andronicus

❦ **I.1** *[Flourish.] Enter the Tribunes and Senators aloft.*
And then enter [below] Saturninus and his Followers
at one door, and Bassianus and his Followers [at the
other], with Drums and Trumpets.

SATURNINUS
Noble patricians, patrons of my right,   1
Defend the justice of my cause with arms.
And countrymen, my loving followers,
Plead my successive title with your swords.   4
I am his first-born son that was the last
That wore the imperial diadem of Rome.
Then let my father's honors live in me,
Nor wrong mine age with this indignity.   8
BASSIANUS
Romans, friends, followers, favorers of my right,
If ever Bassianus, Caesar's son,   10
Were gracious in the eyes of royal Rome,   11
Keep then this passage to the Capitol,   12
And suffer not dishonor to approach
The imperial seat, to virtue consecrate,   14
To justice, continence, and nobility;   15
But let desert in pure election shine,   16

I.1 *Before the Capitol in Rome* **s.d.** *Flourish* trumpet fanfare **1** *patrons* protectors **4** *successive* hereditary **8** *mine age* my status as eldest son **11** *gracious* favored **12** *Keep* guard **14** *consecrate* consecrated, dedicated **15** *continence* self-restraint **16** *let . . . shine* let worth prevail in a free election

And, Romans, fight for freedom in your choice.
[Enter] Marcus Andronicus, [aloft,] with the crown.
MARCUS
Princes that strive by factions and by friends
19   Ambitiously for rule and empery,
20   Know that the people of Rome, for whom we stand
A special party, have by common voice
In election for the Roman empery
23   Chosen Andronicus surnamèd Pius
For many good and great deserts to Rome.
A nobler man, a braver warrior,
Lives not this day within the city walls.
27   He by the Senate is accited home
From weary wars against the barbarous Goths,
29   That with his sons, a terror to our foes,
30   Hath yoked a nation strong, trained up in arms.
Ten years are spent since first he undertook
This cause of Rome, and chastisèd with arms
Our enemies' pride. Five times he hath returned
Bleeding to Rome, bearing his valiant sons
35   In coffins from the field*** and at this day
To the monument of the Andronici
Done sacrifice of expiation
And slain the noblest prisoner of the Goths.***
And now at last, laden with honor's spoils,
40   Returns the good Andronicus to Rome,
Renownèd Titus, flourishing in arms.
42   Let us entreat by honor of his name

---

19 *empery* authority   **23–24** *surnamèd Pius . . . deserts to Rome* given the
honorary title "Pious," "Dutiful," or "Patriotic" for his worthy deeds (*deserts*)
27 *accited* summoned   **29** *That* who   **30** *yoked* conquered   **35–38** *** . . .
*** These three and a half lines, which occur only in Q1, are inconsistent
with the play's action later in I.1. Since Titus has not yet sacrificed Alarbus, it
seems that they either have been misplaced or represent traces of a first draft
mistakenly retained in the printed text.   **42–43** *his name . . . succeed* i.e., the
late emperor, whose successor should be worthy

Whom worthily you would have now succeed,
And in the Capitol and Senate's right,   44
Whom you pretend to honor and adore,   45
That you withdraw you and abate your strength,
Dismiss your followers, and, as suitors should,
Plead your deserts in peace and humbleness.

SATURNINUS
How fair the tribune speaks to calm my thoughts.   49

BASSIANUS
Marcus Andronicus, so I do affy   50
In thy uprightness and integrity,
And so I love and honor thee and thine,
Thy noble brother Titus and his sons,
And her to whom my thoughts are humbled all,   54
Gracious Lavinia, Rome's rich ornament,
That I will here dismiss my loving friends
And to my fortune's and the people's favor
Commit my cause in balance to be weighed.
                                   Exeunt Soldiers [of Bassianus].

SATURNINUS
Friends that have been thus forward in my right,
I thank you all and here dismiss you all,   60
And to the love and favor of my country
Commit myself, my person, and the cause.   62
                              [Exeunt Soldiers of Saturninus.]
Rome, be as just and gracious unto me
As I am confident and kind to thee.   64
Open the gates and let me in.

BASSIANUS
Tribunes, and me, a poor competitor.   66
    [Flourish.] They go up into the Senate House.

---

44 *the Capitol . . . right* the right of the Capitol and of the Senate   45 *pretend* claim   49 *fair* civilly   50 *affy* trust   54 *humbled all* entirely bowed
62 *cause* matter to be decided   64 *confident* trusting; *kind* naturally bound
66 *competitor* rival, co-petitioner

Enter a Captain.

CAPTAIN

Romans, make way. The good Andronicus,
Patron of virtue, Rome's best champion,
Successful in the battles that he fights,
70 With honor and with fortune is returned
71 From where he circumscribèd with his sword
And brought to yoke the enemies of Rome.

Sound Drums and Trumpets, and then enter two of Titus' sons [Martius and Mutius], and then two men bearing a coffin covered with black; then two other sons [Lucius and Quintus]; then Titus Andronicus; and then Tamora, the Queen of Goths, and her two sons, Chiron and Demetrius, with Aaron the Moor, and others as many as can be [including Tamora's son Alarbus and other Goths, prisoners]. Then set down the coffin, and Titus speaks.

TITUS

73 Hail, Rome, victorious in thy mourning weeds!
74 Lo, as the bark that hath discharged her fraught
Returns with precious lading to the bay
76 From whence at first she weighed her anchorage,
Cometh Andronicus, bound with laurel boughs,
To re-salute his country with his tears,
Tears of true joy for his return to Rome.
80 Thou great defender of this Capitol,
Stand gracious to the rites that we intend.
Romans, of five and twenty valiant sons,
83 Half of the number that King Priam had,
Behold the poor remains, alive and dead.
These that survive let Rome reward with love;
86 These that I bring unto their latest home,

---

71 *circumscribèd* rounded up   73 *weeds* clothing   74 *bark . . . fraught* ship that has unloaded her freight   76 *anchorage* anchors   80 *Thou great defender* i.e., Jupiter   83 *King Priam* legendary patriarch of Troy, father of fifty sons   86 *latest* final

With burial amongst their ancestors.
Here Goths have given me leave to sheathe my sword.
Titus, unkind and careless of thine own,   89
Why suffer'st thou thy sons, unburied yet,   90
To hover on the dreadful shore of Styx?   91
Make way to lay them by their brethren.   92
 They open the tomb.
There greet in silence, as the dead are wont,
And sleep in peace, slain in your country's wars.
O sacred receptacle of my joys,
Sweet cell of virtue and nobility,
How many sons hast thou of mine in store
That thou wilt never render to me more!   98

LUCIUS
Give us the proudest prisoner of the Goths,
That we may hew his limbs and on a pile   *100*
Ad manes fratrum sacrifice his flesh   101
Before this earthy prison of their bones,
That so the shadows be not unappeased,   103
Nor we disturbed with prodigies on earth.   104

TITUS
I give him you, the noblest that survives,
The eldest son of this distressèd queen.

TAMORA
Stay, Roman brethren! Gracious conqueror,
Victorious Titus, rue the tears I shed,
A mother's tears in passion for her son: 109
And if thy sons were ever dear to thee,   *110*
O, think my son to be as dear to me!
Sufficeth not that we are brought to Rome
To beautify thy triumphs and return,   113
Captive to thee and to thy Roman yoke,

---

89 *unkind* unnatural 91 *Styx* river surrounding Hades 92 *brethren* (here
the meter indicates the pronunciation "bretheren," as also at ll.351, 360)
98 *more* again 101 *Ad manes fratrum* to the spirits of our brothers (Latin)
103 *shadows* shades, spirits 104 *prodigies* ominous events 109 *passion* grief
113 *triumphs* triumphal processions

But must my sons be slaughtered in the streets
For valiant doings in their country's cause?
O, if to fight for king and commonweal
Were piety in thine, it is in these.
Andronicus, stain not thy tomb with blood.
120   Wilt thou draw near the nature of the gods?
Draw near them then in being merciful.
Sweet mercy is nobility's true badge:
Thrice-noble Titus, spare my first-born son.

TITUS
124   Patient yourself, madam, and pardon me.
These are their brethren whom your Goths beheld
Alive and dead, and for their brethren slain
Religiously they ask a sacrifice.
To this your son is marked, and die he must,
T' appease their groaning shadows that are gone.

LUCIUS
130   Away with him, and make a fire straight,
And with our swords, upon a pile of wood,
Let's hew his limbs till they be clean consumed.
                    Exeunt Titus' sons with Alarbus.

TAMORA
O cruel irreligious piety!

CHIRON
134   Was never Scythia half so barbarous.

DEMETRIUS
135   Oppose not Scythia to ambitious Rome.
Alarbus goes to rest, and we survive
To tremble under Titus' threatening look.
138   Then, madam, stand resolved, but hope withal
139   The selfsame gods that armed the Queen of Troy

---

124 *Patient* calm   130 *straight* immediately, straightaway   134 *Scythia* (ancient name for southern Russia, notorious for its savage people)   135 *Oppose not* do not compare (i.e., Rome is more barbaric)   138 *withal* as well   139–41 *Queen . . . tent* (Hecuba, Queen of Troy, took revenge on Polymnestor, *the Thracian tyrant* who had killed her son, by murdering his sons)

With opportunity of sharp revenge   *140*
Upon the Thracian tyrant in his tent
May favor Tamora, the Queen of Goths
(When Goths were Goths, and Tamora was queen),
To quit the bloody wrongs upon her foes.   144
  Enter the sons of Andronicus again.

LUCIUS
See, lord and father, how we have performed
Our Roman rites. Alarbus' limbs are lopped
And entrails feed the sacrificing fire,
Whose smoke like incense doth perfume the sky.
Remaineth naught but to inter our brethren
And with loud 'larums welcome them to Rome.   150

TITUS
Let it be so, and let Andronicus
Make this his latest farewell to their souls.
  Sound trumpets, and lay the coffin in the tomb.
In peace and honor rest you here, my sons,
Rome's readiest champions, repose you here in rest,
Secure from worldly chances and mishaps.
Here lurks no treason, here no envy swells,   156
Here grow no damnèd drugs, here are no storms,   157
No noise, but silence and eternal sleep.
In peace and honor rest you here, my sons.
  Enter Lavinia.

LAVINIA
In peace and honor live Lord Titus long;   *160*
My noble lord and father, live in fame.
Lo, at this tomb my tributary tears   162
I render for my brethren's obsequies,   163
And at thy feet I kneel, with tears of joy
Shed on this earth for thy return to Rome.
O bless me here with thy victorious hand,

---

144 *quit* requite, revenge   150 *'larums* alarums, trumpet calls   156 *envy*
malice   157 *drugs* poisonous plants   162 *tributary* offered as tribute   163
obsequies funeral rites

Whose fortunes Rome's best citizens applaud.

TITUS
Kind Rome, that hast thus lovingly reserved
169   The cordial of mine age to glad my heart.
170   Lavinia, live; outlive thy father's days,
And fame's eternal date, for virtue's praise.

MARCUS   *[Aloft]*
Long live Lord Titus, my belovèd brother,
Gracious triumpher in the eyes of Rome!

TITUS
Thanks, gentle tribune, noble brother Marcus.

MARCUS
And welcome, nephews, from successful wars,
You that survive, and you that sleep in fame.
Fair lords, your fortunes are alike in all
That in your country's service drew your swords;
But safer triumph is this funeral pomp
180   That hath aspired to Solon's happiness
And triumphs over chance in honor's bed.
Titus Andronicus, the people of Rome,
Whose friend in justice thou hast ever been,
Send thee by me, their tribune and their trust,
185   This palliament of white and spotless hue,
186   And name thee in election for the empire,
With these our late-deceasèd emperor's sons.
188   Be *candidatus* then, and put it on,
And help to set a head on headless Rome.

TITUS
190   A better head her glorious body fits
Than his that shakes for age and feebleness.
192   What should I don this robe, and trouble you?
Be chosen with proclamations today,

---

169 *cordial* comfort   180 *aspired* risen; *Solon's happiness* (Solon, the Greek legislator and sage, said "Call no man happy until he is dead")   185 *palliament* robe   186 *in election* i.e., as a candidate   188 *candidatus* candidate (Latin, literally "white-robed")   192 *What* why

Tomorrow yield up rule, resign my life,
And set abroad new business for you all?   195
Rome, I have been thy soldier forty years,
And led my country's strength successfully,
And buried one and twenty valiant sons,
Knighted in field, slain manfully in arms,
In right and service of their noble country.   200
Give me a staff of honor for mine age,
But not a scepter to control the world.
Upright he held it, lords, that held it last.

MARCUS
Titus, thou shalt obtain and ask the empery.   204

SATURNINUS
Proud and ambitious tribune, canst thou tell?   205

TITUS
Patience, Prince Saturninus.

SATURNINUS   Romans, do me right.
Patricians, draw your swords, and sheathe them not
Till Saturninus be Rome's emperor.
Andronicus, would thou were shipped to hell
Rather than rob me of the people's hearts!   210

LUCIUS
Proud Saturnine, interrupter of the good
That noble-minded Titus means to thee!

TITUS
Content thee, prince, I will restore to thee
The people's hearts, and wean them from themselves.

BASSIANUS
Andronicus, I do not flatter thee,
But honor thee, and will do till I die.
My faction if thou strengthen with thy friends,
I will most thankful be, and thanks to men
Of noble minds is honorable meed.   219

---

195 *set abroad* initiate 204 *obtain and ask* i.e., obtain merely by asking
205 *canst thou tell* i.e., Oh, really? Are you sure? 219 *meed* reward

TITUS
220   People of Rome, and people's tribunes here,
221   I ask your voices and your suffrages.
       Will ye bestow them friendly on Andronicus?
TRIBUNES
       To gratify the good Andronicus,
224   And gratulate his safe return to Rome,
225   The people will accept whom he admits.
TITUS
       Tribunes, I thank you, and this suit I make,
227   That you create our emperor's eldest son,
       Lord Saturnine, whose virtues will, I hope,
229   Reflect on Rome as Titan's rays on earth,
230   And ripen justice in this commonweal.
       Then if you will elect by my advice,
       Crown him and say "Long live our emperor!"
MARCUS
233   With voices and applause of every sort,
       Patricians and plebeians, we create
       Lord Saturninus Rome's great emperor
       And say "Long live our emperor Saturnine!"
       [A long flourish till they come down.]
SATURNINUS
       Titus Andronicus, for thy favors done
238   To us in our election this day
239   I give thee thanks in part of thy deserts,
240   And will with deeds requite thy gentleness:
241   And for an onset, Titus, to advance
       Thy name and honorable family,
243   Lavinia will I make my empress,

---

221 *suffrages* votes   224 *gratulate* rejoice at   225 *admits* selects, literally "allows to enter"   227 *create* invest with title   229 *Titan* the sun god   233 *of
every sort* from all classes   238 *election* (here, as frequently in Shakespeare,
the "ion" is pronounced as two syllables)   239 *in part of* i.e., as partial reward for   241 *onset* beginning   243 *empress* (here the meter indicates that
the word is pronounced as three syllables, "em-per-ess"; at other times it is
pronounced as two, "em-press")

Rome's royal mistress, mistress of my heart,
And in the sacred Pantheon her espouse.   245
Tell me, Andronicus, doth this motion please thee?   246

TITUS
It doth, my worthy lord, and in this match
I hold me highly honored of your grace;
And here in sight of Rome, to Saturnine,
King and commander of our commonweal,   250
The wide world's emperor, do I consecrate
My sword, my chariot, and my prisoners,
Presents well worthy Rome's imperious lord.   253
Receive them then, the tribute that I owe,
Mine honor's ensigns humbled at thy feet.   255

SATURNINUS
Thanks, noble Titus, father of my life.
How proud I am of thee and of thy gifts
Rome shall record, and when I do forget
The least of these unspeakable deserts,   259
Romans, forget your fealty to me.   260

TITUS *[To Tamora]*
Now, madam, are you prisoner to an emperor,
To him that for your honor and your state   262
Will use you nobly and your followers.   263

SATURNINUS *[Aside]*
A goodly lady, trust me, of the hue   264
That I would choose, were I to choose anew. –
Clear up, fair queen, that cloudy countenance.
Though chance of war hath wrought this change of   267
  cheer,
Thou com'st not to be made a scorn in Rome.
Princely shall be thy usage every way.
Rest on my word, and let not discontent   270

---

245 *Pantheon* Roman temple dedicated to all the gods   246 *motion* proposal
253 *imperious* imperial   255 *ensigns* symbols   259 *unspeakable* inexpressible
260 *fealty* loyalty   262 *for* because of; *state* position   263 *use* treat   264 *hue*
appearance, species (but the modern sense of "color" is pertinent to the
image patterns of the play)   267 *cheer* countenance

271 Daunt all your hopes. Madam, he comforts you
     Can make you greater than the Queen of Goths.
     Lavinia, you are not displeased with this?
LAVINIA
274 Not I, my lord, sith true nobility
275 Warrants these words in princely courtesy.
SATURNINUS
     Thanks, sweet Lavinia. Romans, let us go.
     Ransomless here we set our prisoners free.
     Proclaim our honors, lords, with trump and drum.
                    [Flourish. Exeunt Saturninus, Tamora,
                        Demetrius, Chiron, and Aaron.]
BASSIANUS
     Lord Titus, by your leave, this maid is mine.
        [Seizes Lavinia.]
TITUS
280 How, sir! Are you in earnest then, my lord?
BASSIANUS
     Ay, noble Titus, and resolved withal
     To do myself this reason and this right.
MARCUS
283 *Suum cuique* is our Roman justice:
     This prince in justice seizeth but his own.
LUCIUS
     And that he will, and shall if Lucius live.
TITUS
286 Traitors, avaunt! Where is the emperor's guard?
287 Treason, my lord! Lavinia is surprised!
SATURNINUS *[Reentering]*
     Surprised? By whom?
BASSIANUS   By him that justly may
     Bear his betrothed from all the world away.
                    [Exeunt Bassianus and Marcus with Lavinia.]

---

271 *he* i.e., the man who   274 *sith* since   275 *Warrants* justifies   283 *Suum
cuique* to each his own (Latin)   286 *avaunt* be off   287 *surprised* taken captive

MUTIUS

   Brothers, help to convey her hence away,   *290*

   And with my sword I'll keep this door safe.   *291*

        [Exeunt Lucius, Quintus, and Martius.]

TITUS

   Follow, my lord, and I'll soon bring her back.

                [Exit Saturninus.]

MUTIUS

   My lord, you pass not here.

TITUS   What, villain boy?

   Barr'st me my way in Rome?

MUTIUS   Help, Lucius, help!

   [Titus kills him.]

   [Enter Lucius.]

LUCIUS

   My lord, you are unjust, and more than so,

   In wrongful quarrel you have slain your son.

TITUS

   Nor thou, nor he, are any sons of mine;   *297*

   My sons would never so dishonor me.

   Enter aloft the Emperor with Tamora and her two

   sons, and Aaron the Moor.

   Traitor, restore Lavinia to the emperor.

LUCIUS

   Dead, if you will, but not to be his wife,   *300*

   That is another's lawful promised love.   *[Exit.]*

SATURNINUS

   No, Titus, no. The emperor needs her not,

   Nor her, nor thee, nor any of thy stock.

   I'll trust by leisure him that mocks me once;   *304*

   Thee never, nor thy traitorous haughty sons,

   Confederates all thus to dishonor me.

   Was none in Rome to make a stale   *307*

---

291 *door* (pronounced as two syllables) **297** *Nor . . . nor* neither . . . nor
304 *by leisure* cautiously **307** *Was none . . . stale* was there no one to make a
laughingstock of

But Saturnine? Full well, Andronicus,
Agree these deeds with that proud brag of thine
310   That said'st I begged the empire at thy hands.

TITUS

O monstrous! What reproachful words are these?

SATURNINUS

312   But go thy ways; go, give that changing piece
To him that flourished for her with his sword.
A valiant son-in-law thou shalt enjoy,
315   One fit to bandy with thy lawless sons,
316   To ruffle in the commonwealth of Rome.

TITUS

These words are razors to my wounded heart.

SATURNINUS

And therefore, lovely Tamora, Queen of Goths,
319   That like the stately Phoebe 'mongst her nymphs
320   Dost overshine the gallantest dames of Rome,
If thou be pleased with this my sudden choice,
Behold, I choose thee, Tamora, for my bride
And will create thee Empress of Rome.
Speak, Queen of Goths, dost thou applaud my choice?
And here I swear by all the Roman gods,
Sith priest and holy water are so near,
And tapers burn so bright, and everything
328   In readiness for Hymenaeus stand,
I will not re-salute the streets of Rome
330   Or climb my palace till from forth this place
I lead espoused my bride along with me.

TAMORA

And here in sight of heaven to Rome I swear,
If Saturnine advance the Queen of Goths,
She will a handmaid be to his desires,

---

312 *changing piece* fickle woman (the phrase suggests a coin passed from man to man; also "piece of flesh" or its modern equivalent)   315 *bandy* brawl 316 *ruffle* swagger   319 *Phoebe* the moon goddess   328 *Hymenaeus* god of marriage

A loving nurse, a mother to his youth.

SATURNINUS

Ascend, fair queen, Pantheon. Lords, accompany
Your noble emperor and his lovely bride,
Sent by the heavens for Prince Saturnine,
Whose wisdom hath her fortune conquerèd.
There shall we consummate our spousal rites.   340

Exeunt omnes [Titus remains].

TITUS

I am not bid to wait upon this bride.   341
Titus, when wert thou wont to walk alone,
Dishonored thus and challengèd of wrongs?   343

*Enter Marcus and Titus' sons [Lucius, Quintus, and
Martius].*

MARCUS

O Titus, see, O see what thou hast done,
In a bad quarrel slain a virtuous son.

TITUS

No, foolish tribune, no: no son of mine,
Nor thou, nor these, confederates in the deed
That hath dishonored all our family,
Unworthy brother, and unworthy sons!

LUCIUS

But let us give him burial as becomes,   350
Give Mutius burial with our brethren.

TITUS

Traitors, away! He rests not in this tomb:
This monument five hundred years hath stood,
Which I have sumptuously reedified.   354
Here none but soldiers and Rome's servitors   355
Repose in fame; none basely slain in brawls.
Bury him where you can, he comes not here.

MARCUS

My lord, this is impiety in you.

---

341 *bid* asked **343** *challengèd* accused **350** *becomes* is fitting **354**
reedified rebuilt **355** *servitors* officers

My nephew Mutius' deeds do plead for him;
360 He must be buried with his brethren.
　　　Titus' two sons speak.
[QUINTUS, MARTIUS]
　　And shall, or him we will accompany.
TITUS
　　And shall? What villain was it spake that word?
　　　Titus' son speaks.
[QUINTUS]
363 He that would vouch it in any place but here.
TITUS
364 What, would you bury him in my despite?
MARCUS
　　No, noble Titus, but entreat of thee
　　To pardon Mutius and to bury him.
TITUS
　　Marcus, even thou hast struck upon my crest,
　　And with these boys mine honor thou hast wounded.
369 My foes I do repute you every one,
370 So trouble me no more, but get you gone.
MARTIUS
371 He is not with himself, let us withdraw.
QUINTUS
　　Not I, till Mutius' bones be burièd.
　　　The brother and the sons kneel.
MARCUS
　　Brother, for in that name doth nature plead –
QUINTUS
　　Father, and in that name doth nature speak –
TITUS
375 Speak thou no more, if all the rest will speed.
MARCUS
　　Renownèd Titus, more than half my soul –

---

363 *vouch* maintain　**364** *in my despite* in spite of me　**369** *repute* consider
371 *with himself* in his right mind　**375** *if . . . speed* i.e., if you (the remaining sons) hope to stay alive

LUCIUS
   Dear father, soul and substance of us all –
MARCUS
   Suffer thy brother Marcus to inter   378
   His noble nephew here in virtue's nest,
   That died in honor and Lavinia's cause.   380
   Thou art a Roman, be not barbarous:
   The Greeks upon advice did bury Ajax,   382
   That slew himself; and wise Laertes' son   383
   Did graciously plead for his funerals.
   Let not young Mutius then, that was thy joy,
   Be barred his entrance here.
TITUS   Rise, Marcus, rise.
   The dismallest day is this that e'er I saw,
   To be dishonored by my sons in Rome.
   Well, bury him, and bury me the next.
   They put him in the tomb.

LUCIUS
   There lie thy bones, sweet Mutius, with thy friends,   390
   Till we with trophies do adorn thy tomb.   391
   They all kneel and say:
[ALL]
   No man shed tears for noble Mutius;
   He lives in fame that died in virtue's cause.
   Exeunt [i.e., stand aside] all but Marcus and Titus.
MARCUS
   My lord, to step out of these dreary dumps,   394
   How comes it that the subtle Queen of Goths
   Is of a sudden thus advanced in Rome?
TITUS
   I know not, Marcus, but I know it is:
   Whether by device or no, the heavens can tell.   398

---

378 *Suffer* permit 382 *advice* deliberation; *Ajax* (Ajax killed himself in fury because the armor of Achilles was awarded to Odysseus) 383 *Laertes' son* Odysseus 391 *trophies* memorial tokens 394 *dumps* i.e., melancholy 398 *device* plot

399 Is she not then beholding to the man
400 That brought her for this high good turn so far?
401 [Yes, and will nobly him remunerate.]

> *[Flourish.] Enter the Emperor, Tamora and her two*
> *sons, with the Moor, at one door. Enter at the other*
> *door Bassianus and Lavinia, with others.*

SATURNINUS

402 So, Bassianus, you have played your prize.
God give you joy, sir, of your gallant bride.

BASSIANUS

And you of yours, my lord. I say no more
Nor wish no less, and so I take my leave.

SATURNINUS

Traitor, if Rome have law or we have power,
407 Thou and thy faction shall repent this rape.

BASSIANUS

Rape call you it, my lord, to seize my own,
My true betrothèd love, and now my wife?
410 But let the laws of Rome determine all;
411 Meanwhile am I possessed of that is mine.

SATURNINUS

'Tis good, sir. You are very short with us,
But if we live, we'll be as sharp with you.

BASSIANUS

My lord, what I have done, as best I may
Answer I must, and shall do with my life.
Only thus much I give your grace to know:
By all the duties that I owe to Rome,
This noble gentleman, Lord Titus here,
419 Is in opinion and in honor wronged,
420 That in the rescue of Lavinia
With his own hand did slay his youngest son,
In zeal to you, and highly moved to wrath

---

399 *beholding* indebted   401 (line printed only in F; some editors assign it
to Marcus)   402 *played your prize* won your match (fencing term)   407
rape seizure (of Lavinia)   411 *that* that which   419 *opinion* reputation

To be controlled in that he frankly gave.   423
Receive him then to favor, Saturnine,
That hath expressed himself in all his deeds
A father and a friend to thee and Rome.

TITUS

Prince Bassianus, leave to plead my deeds.   427
'Tis thou, and those, that have dishonored me.
Rome and the righteous heavens be my judge
How I have loved and honored Saturnine.   *430*

TAMORA

My worthy lord, if ever Tamora
Were gracious in those princely eyes of thine,
Then hear me speak indifferently for all,   433
And at my suit, sweet, pardon what is past.

SATURNINUS

What, madam, be dishonored openly
And basely put it up without revenge?   436

TAMORA

Not so, my lord; the gods of Rome forfend   437
I should be author to dishonor you!   438
But on mine honor dare I undertake   439
For good Lord Titus' innocence in all,   440
Whose fury not dissembled speaks his griefs: 441
Then at my suit look graciously on him.
Lose not so noble a friend on vain suppose,   443
Nor with sour looks afflict his gentle heart.
   [Aside to Saturninus]
My lord, be ruled by me, be won at last,
Dissemble all your griefs and discontents:
You are but newly planted in your throne;
Lest, then, the people, and patricians too,
Upon a just survey take Titus' part,

---

423 *controlled* thwarted; *frankly* freely   **427** *leave to plead* refrain from pleading   **433** *indifferently* impartially   **436** *put it up* accept it   **437** *forfend* forbid   **438** *author* agent   **439** *undertake* vouch   **441** i.e., whose undisguised rage attests to his grievances   **443** *vain suppose* idle supposition

450 And so supplant you for ingratitude,
Which Rome reputes to be a heinous sin,
452 Yield at entreats: and then let me alone,
I'll find a day to massacre them all
454 And race their faction and their family,
The cruel father, and his traitorous sons,
To whom I suèd for my dear son's life,
And make them know what 'tis to let a queen
Kneel in the streets and beg for grace in vain.
    [Aloud]
Come, come, sweet emperor – come, Andronicus –
460 Take up this good old man, and cheer the heart
That dies in tempest of thy angry frown.

SATURNINUS
Rise, Titus, rise, my empress hath prevailed.

TITUS
I thank your majesty, and her, my lord.
These words, these looks, infuse new life in me.

TAMORA
465 Titus, I am incorporate in Rome,
A Roman now adopted happily,
And must advise the emperor for his good.
This day all quarrels die, Andronicus.
And let it be mine honor, good my lord,
470 That I have reconciled your friends and you.
For you, Prince Bassianus, I have passed
My word and promise to the emperor
That you will be more mild and tractable.
And fear not, lords, and you, Lavinia;
By my advice, all humbled on your knees
You shall ask pardon of his majesty.
    [They kneel.]

---

452 *at entreats* to entreaty; *let me alone* leave it to me   454 *race* eradicate
465 *am incorporate in* have become a part of

LUCIUS
  We do, and vow to heaven and to his highness
  That what we did was mildly as we might,   478
  Tendering our sister's honor and our own.   479
MARCUS
  That on mine honor here do I protest.   480
SATURNINUS
  Away, and talk not, trouble us no more.
TAMORA
  Nay, nay, sweet emperor, we must all be friends.
  The tribune and his nephews kneel for grace.
  I will not be denied. Sweet heart, look back.
SATURNINUS
  Marcus, for thy sake and thy brother's here,
  And at my lovely Tamora's entreats,
  I do remit these young men's heinous faults.
  Stand up.
    [They rise.]
  Lavinia, though you left me like a churl,   489
  I found a friend; and sure as death I swore   490
  I would not part a bachelor from the priest.   491
  Come, if the emperor's court can feast two brides,
  You are my guest, Lavinia, and your friends.
  This day shall be a love-day, Tamora.   494
TITUS
  Tomorrow, an it please your majesty   495
  To hunt the panther and the hart with me,
  With horn and hound we'll give your grace *bon jour*.   497
SATURNINUS
  Be it so, Titus, and gramercy too.   498
              Exeunt. Sound trumpets. Manet [Aaron the] Moor.
                            ✳

---

478 *mildly . . . might* as mild as might be (i.e., in the circumstances)   479
Tendering having regard for   480 *protest* declare   489 *like a churl* rudely, un-
generously   491 *part* depart   494 *love-day* day appointed to settle disputes
(with pun on "day of love")   495 *an* if   497 *bon jour* good day   498
gramercy thanks

❧ II.1

AARON

1   Now climbeth Tamora Olympus' top,
     Safe out of fortune's shot, and sits aloft,
3   Secure of thunder's crack or lightning flash,
     Advanced above pale envy's threatening reach.
     As when the golden sun salutes the morn,
     And having gilt the ocean with his beams,
7   Gallops the zodiac in his glistering coach
8   And overlooks the highest-peering hills,
     So Tamora.
10   Upon her wit doth earthly honor wait,
     And virtue stoops and trembles at her frown.
     Then, Aaron, arm thy heart and fit thy thoughts
     To mount aloft with thy imperial mistress,
14   And mount her pitch whom thou in triumph long
15   Hast prisoner held, fettered in amorous chains,
16   And faster bound to Aaron's charming eyes
17   Than is Prometheus tied to Caucasus.
18   Away with slavish weeds and servile thoughts!
     I will be bright and shine in pearl and gold,
20   To wait upon this new-made empress.
21   To wait, said I? to wanton with this queen,
22   This goddess, this Semiramis, this nymph,
     This siren that will charm Rome's Saturnine

II.1 (There is no break in the action, since Aaron remains onstage.) **1** *Olympus* Mount Olympus, home of the gods **3** *of* from **7** *Gallops* gallops through **8** *overlooks* looks down upon **14** *mount her pitch* rise to the highest point of her flight (a term from falconry, but with the sexual connotation of "mount," as in l. 13) **15** *fettered* bound **16** *charming* casting a magic spell **17** *Prometheus* (one of the Titans, who stole fire from heaven; as punishment, Zeus chained him to Mount Caucasus) **18** *weeds* garments **21** *to wanton* to sport sexually **22** *Semiramis* (legendary Assyrian queen, renowned for her beauty and sexuality)

And see his shipwrack and his commonweal's.
Holla! what storm is this?   25
   Enter Chiron and Demetrius, braving.

DEMETRIUS
Chiron, thy years wants wit, thy wits wants edge   26
And manners, to intrude where I am graced   27
And may, for aught thou knowest, affected be.   28

CHIRON
Demetrius, thou dost overween in all,   29
And so in this, to bear me down with braves.   30
'Tis not the difference of a year or two
Makes me less gracious, or thee more fortunate:
I am as able and as fit as thou
To serve, and to deserve my mistress' grace,
And that my sword upon thee shall approve,   35
And plead my passions for Lavinia's love.

AARON
Clubs, clubs! These lovers will not keep the peace.   37

DEMETRIUS
Why, boy, although our mother, unadvised,   38
Gave you a dancing rapier by your side,   39
Are you so desperate grown to threat your friends?   40
Go to! Have your lath glued within your sheath   41
Till you know better how to handle it.

CHIRON
Meanwhile, sir, with the little skill I have,
Full well shalt thou perceive how much I dare.

DEMETRIUS
Ay, boy, grow ye so brave?

------

25 s.d. *braving* talking loudly and arrogantly, swaggering 26 *wants* lacks
(the ending "-s" is sometimes used with a plural subject); *edge* sharpness 27
graced favored 28 *affected* loved 29 *overween* presume too much 30
braves threats 35 *approve* prove 37 *Clubs, clubs* (cry associated with brawl-
ing apprentices in Elizabethan London; Aaron mocks the brothers' adoles-
cent vulgarity) 38 *unadvised* unwisely 39 *dancing rapier* ornamental
sword worn by dancers 41 *Go to!* (expression of impatience – "Come on!");
lath wooden stage sword (contemptuous)

They draw.

AARON   Why, how now, lords?
  So near the emperor's palace dare ye draw
  And maintain such a quarrel openly?
48 Full well I wot the ground of all this grudge:
  I would not for a million of gold
50 The cause were known to them it most concerns,
  Nor would your noble mother for much more
  Be so dishonored in the court of Rome.
53 For shame, put up.

DEMETRIUS   Not I, till I have sheathed
  My rapier in his bosom, and withal
  Thrust those reproachful speeches down his throat
  That he hath breathed in my dishonor here.

CHIRON
  For that I am prepared and full resolved,
  Foul-spoken coward, that thunderest with thy tongue
  And with thy weapon nothing dar'st perform.

AARON
60 Away, I say!
  Now, by the gods that warlike Goths adore,
62 This petty brabble will undo us all.
  Why, lords, and think you not how dangerous
64 It is to jet upon a prince's right?
  What, is Lavinia then become so loose,
  Or Bassianus so degenerate,
  That for her love such quarrels may be broached
  Without controlment, justice, or revenge?
  Young lords, beware! and should the empress know
70 This discord's ground, the music would not please.

CHIRON
  I care not, I, knew she and all the world:
  I love Lavinia more than all the world.

---

48 *wot* know   53 *put up* sheathe your swords   62 *brabble* brawl   64 *jet* en-
croach   70 *ground* reason (with a pun on the musical sense "bass line")

DEMETRIUS
    Youngling, learn thou to make some meaner choice.   73
    Lavinia is thine elder brother's hope.
AARON
    Why, are ye mad? or know ye not in Rome
    How furious and impatient they be,
    And cannot brook competitors in love?   77
    I tell you, lords, you do but plot your deaths
    By this device.
CHIRON   Aaron, a thousand deaths
    Would I propose to achieve her whom I love.   80
AARON
    To achieve her! How?   81
DEMETRIUS   Why makes thou it so strange?
    She is a woman, therefore may be wooed;
    She is a woman, therefore may be won;
    She is Lavinia, therefore must be loved.
    What, man! more water glideth by the mill
    Than wots the miller of, and easy it is
    Of a cut loaf to steal a shive, we know: 87
    Though Bassianus be the emperor's brother,
    Better than he have worn Vulcan's badge.   89
AARON   *[Aside]*
    Ay, and as good as Saturninus may.   *90*
DEMETRIUS
    Then why should he despair that knows to court it
    With words, fair looks, and liberality?
    What, hast not thou full often struck a doe,   93
    And borne her cleanly by the keeper's nose?
AARON
    Why, then, it seems some certain snatch or so   95

---

73 *Youngling* youngster (contemptuous); *meaner* lower (socially)   77 *brook* tolerate   80 *propose* be ready to face   81 *Why . . . strange?* why do you seem so surprised   87 *shive* slice   89 *Vulcan's badge* cuckold's horns, sign of a betrayed husband (Vulcan, god of fire, was deceived by his wife, Venus)   93 *struck* shot (with an arrow)   95 *snatch* quick copulation, with the sense of "snack" or "fast bite"

96   Would serve your turns.

CHIRON   Ay, so the turn were served.

DEMETRIUS

97   Aaron, thou hast hit it.

AARON   Would you had hit it too!
      Then should not we be tired with this ado.
      Why, hark ye, hark ye, and are you such fools

100   To square for this? Would it offend you then
101   That both should speed?

CHIRON
      Faith, not me.

DEMETRIUS   Nor me, so I were one.

AARON

103   For shame, be friends, and join for that you jar.
104   'Tis policy and stratagem must do
105   That you affect; and so must you resolve,
      That what you cannot as you would achieve,
      You must perforce accomplish as you may.

108   Take this of me: Lucrece was not more chaste
      Than this Lavinia, Bassianus' love.

110   A speedier course than lingering languishment
      Must we pursue, and I have found the path.

112   My lords, a solemn hunting is in hand;
      There will the lovely Roman ladies troop:
      The forest walks are wide and spacious,

115   And many unfrequented plots there are,
116   Fitted by kind for rape and villainy.
117   Single you thither then this dainty doe,
      And strike her home by force, if not by words.
      This way, or not at all, stand you in hope.

---

96 *turns* purposes (with sexual meaning)   97 *hit it* got it, with sexual meaning ("scored") in Aaron's reply   100 *square* quarrel   101 *speed* succeed (again, sexually)   103 *join . . . jar* unite to get what you quarrel over   104 *policy* cunning   105 *affect* desire   108 *Lucrece* chaste Roman matron whose rape by Tarquin and subsequent suicide is the subject of Shakespeare's poem *The Rape of Lucrece*   110 *languishment* lovesickness   112 *solemn* ceremonial   115 *plots* places   116 *kind* nature   117 *Single* single out (a hunting term)

Come, come, our empress, with her sacred wit   *120*
To villainy and vengeance consecrate,
Will we acquaint withal what we intend;
And she shall file our engines with advice,   *123*
That will not suffer you to square yourselves,
But to your wishes' height advance you both.
The emperor's court is like the house of fame,   *126*
The palace full of tongues, of eyes and ears:
The woods are ruthless, dreadful, deaf, and dull.   *128*
There speak and strike, brave boys, and take your
     turns,
There serve your lust, shadowed from heaven's eye,   *130*
And revel in Lavinia's treasury.

CHIRON
Thy counsel, lad, smells of no cowardice.

DEMETRIUS
Sit fas aut nefas, till I find the stream   *133*
To cool this heat, a charm to calm these fits,
Per Stygia, per manes vehor.   *Exeunt.* *135*

                       *

～ **II.2** *Enter Titus Andronicus and his three sons [and
    Marcus], making a noise with hounds and horns.*

TITUS
The hunt is up, the morn is bright and gray,
The fields are fragrant and the woods are green.
Uncouple here and let us make a bay,   *3*
And wake the emperor and his lovely bride,
And rouse the prince, and ring a hunter's peal,

---

123 *file our engines* sharpen our schemes   **126** *house of fame* home of rumor
(a possible glance at Chaucer's poem *The House of Fame*)   **128** *ruthless* pitiless   **133** *Sit . . . nefas* be it right or wrong (Latin)   **135** *Per . . . vehor* I am
borne through the Stygian (hellish) realms (Latin)
     II.2 The grounds of the emperor's palace   **3** *Uncouple* unleash the
hounds; *bay* prolonged barking

That all the court may echo with the noise.
Sons, let it be your charge, as it is ours,
To attend the emperor's person carefully:
I have been troubled in my sleep this night,

10   But dawning day new comfort hath inspired.
        Here a cry of hounds, and wind horns in a peal, then
        enter Saturninus, Tamora, Bassianus, Lavinia,
        Chiron, Demetrius, and their Attendants.
      Many good morrows to your majesty!
      Madam, to you as many and as good!
      I promisèd your grace a hunter's peal.
SATURNINUS
    And you have rung it lustily, my lords,
    Somewhat too early for new-married ladies.
BASSIANUS
    Lavinia, how say you?
LAVINIA   I say, no:
    I have been broad awake two hours and more.
SATURNINUS
    Come on then, horse and chariots let us have,
    And to our sport. Madam, now shall ye see
20   Our Roman hunting.
MARCUS   I have dogs, my lord,
21 Will rouse the proudest panther in the chase,
    And climb the highest promontory top.
TITUS
    And I have horse will follow where the game
    Makes way and runs like swallows o'er the plain.
DEMETRIUS
    Chiron, we hunt not, we, with horse nor hound,
    But hope to pluck a dainty doe to ground.   *Exeunt.*
                        ✳

---

21 *chase* hunting ground

∾ **II.3** *Enter Aaron alone [with a bag of gold].*

AARON
He that had wit would think that I had none,
To bury so much gold under a tree,
And never after to inherit it.   3
Let him that thinks of me so abjectly
Know that this gold must coin a stratagem,   5
Which, cunningly effected, will beget
A very excellent piece of villainy:
And so repose, sweet gold, for their unrest   8
   [Hides the gold.]
That have their alms out of the empress' chest.
   Enter Tamora alone to the Moor.
TAMORA
My lovely Aaron, wherefore look'st thou sad   10
When everything doth make a gleeful boast?   11
The birds chaunt melody on every bush,
The snake lies rollèd in the cheerful sun,
The green leaves quiver with the cooling wind,
And make a checkered shadow on the ground;
Under their sweet shade, Aaron, let us sit,
And whilst the babbling echo mocks the hounds,
Replying shrilly to the well-tuned horns,
As if a double hunt were heard at once,
Let us sit down and mark their yellowing noise;   20
And after conflict such as was supposed
The wandering prince and Dido once enjoyed,   22
When with a happy storm they were surprised,
And curtained with a counsel-keeping cave,   24

II.3 A forest near Rome   **3** *inherit* possess   **5** *coin* produce (as in coining money)   **8–9** *their unrest . . . chest* the distress of those who find this money belonging to the empress   **11** *boast* display   **20** *yellowing* bellowing   **22** *wandering prince* Aeneas, Trojan hero who loved Dido, Queen of Carthage   **24** *counsel-keeping* private

We may, each wreathèd in the other's arms,
Our pastimes done, possess a golden slumber,
Whiles hounds and horns and sweet melodious birds
Be unto us as is a nurse's song
Of lullaby to bring her babe asleep.

AARON

30   Madam, though Venus govern your desires,
31   Saturn is dominator over mine.
32   What signifies my deadly-standing eye,
      My silence, and my cloudy melancholy,
      My fleece of woolly hair that now uncurls
      Even as an adder when she doth unroll
      To do some fatal execution?
37   No, madam, these are no venereal signs.
      Vengeance is in my heart, death in my hand,
39   Blood and revenge are hammering in my head.
40   Hark, Tamora, the empress of my soul,
      Which never hopes more heaven than rests in thee,
      This is the day of doom for Bassianus;
43   His Philomel must lose her tongue today,
      Thy sons make pillage of her chastity
      And wash their hands in Bassianus' blood.
      Seest thou this letter? take it up, I pray thee,
47   And give the king this fatal-plotted scroll.
      Now question me no more, we are espied;
49   Here comes a parcel of our hopeful booty,
50   Which dreads not yet their lives' destruction.
          Enter Bassianus and Lavinia.

───────

31 *dominator* the planet that has a dominant place in the horoscope (people dominated by Saturn were reputedly of sluggish, cold, and gloomy temperament) **32** *deadly-standing* death-dealing **37** *venereal* amorous (the word derives from Venus, goddess of love) **39** *hammering* beating, but also agitating, debating with each other **43** *Philomel* (in Greek myth Tereus raped Philomel and cut out her tongue, but she accused him by weaving the story into a tapestry; see also II.4.26–27, 38–43; IV.1.47–48; V.2.194) **47** *fatal-plotted* devised to kill **49** *parcel . . . booty* part of the prize we hope for

TAMORA
  Ah, my sweet Moor, sweeter to me than life.

AARON
  No more, great empress; Bassianus comes.
  Be cross with him, and I'll go fetch thy sons
  To back thy quarrels, whatsoe'er they be.   *[Exit.]*

BASSIANUS
  Who have we here? Rome's royal empress,
  Unfurnished of her well-beseeming troop?   56
  Or is it Dian, habited like her,   57
  Who hath abandonèd her holy groves
  To see the general hunting in this forest?

TAMORA
  Saucy controller of my private steps!   60
  Had I the power that some say Dian had,
  Thy temples should be planted presently   62
  With horns, as was Actaeon's, and the hounds   63
  Should drive upon thy new-transformèd limbs,   64
  Unmannerly intruder as thou art!

LAVINIA
  Under your patience, gentle empress,
  'Tis thought you have a goodly gift in horning,   67
  And to be doubted that your Moor and you   68
  Are singled forth to try experiments.   69
  Jove shield your husband from his hounds today!   70
  'Tis pity they should take him for a stag.

BASSIANUS
  Believe me, queen, your swart Cimmerian   72

---

56 *Unfurnished of* deprived of; *well-beseeming* appropriate **57** *Dian* Diana, goddess of hunting and chastity; *habited* dressed **60** *Saucy controller* rude monitor **62** *presently* immediately **63** *Actaeon* (legendary hunter who spied on Diana as she bathed; she transformed him into a stag, and his own hounds killed him) **64** *drive* rush **67** *horning* adultery, giving a husband horns **68** *doubted* suspected **69** *try experiments* experiment sexually **72** *swart Cimmerian* (a double racial insult: *swart* means "black," and the legendary Cimmerians lived in darkness)

Doth make your honor of his body's hue,
Spotted, detested, and abominable.
Why are you sequestered from all your train,
Dismounted from your snow-white goodly steed,
And wandered hither to an obscure plot,
Accompanied but with a barbarous Moor,
If foul desire had not conducted you?

LAVINIA

80   And being intercepted in your sport,
81   Great reason that my noble lord be rated
       For sauciness. I pray you let us hence,
83   And let her joy her raven-colored love;
       This valley fits the purpose passing well.

BASSIANUS

The king my brother shall have note of this.

LAVINIA

86   Ay, for these slips have made him noted long.
       Good king, to be so mightily abused!

TAMORA

Why, I have patience to endure all this.
       Enter Chiron and Demetrius.

DEMETRIUS

How now, dear sovereign and our gracious mother,
90   Why doth your highness look so pale and wan?

TAMORA

Have I not reason, think you, to look pale?
92   These two have ticed me hither to this place,
       A barren detested vale you see it is;
       The trees, though summer, yet forlorn and lean,
95   Overcome with moss and baleful mistletoe.
       Here never shines the sun, here nothing breeds,

---

81 *rated* berated, scolded   83 *joy* enjoy   86 *slips* offenses; *noted long* notorious for some time, playing on "note" in the previous line (either Shakespeare deliberately ignores the actual time scheme or this passage is evidence of unrevised text)   92 *ticed* enticed   95 *Overcome* overgrown; *baleful* deadly

Unless the nightly owl or fatal raven: 97
And when they showed me this abhorrèd pit,
They told me, here, at dead time of the night,
A thousand fiends, a thousand hissing snakes,   *100*
Ten thousand swelling toads, as many urchins,   101
Would make such fearful and confusèd cries
As any mortal body hearing it
Should straight fall mad, or else die suddenly.
No sooner had they told this hellish tale
But straight they told me they would bind me here
Unto the body of a dismal yew
And leave me to this miserable death;
And then they called me foul adulteress,
Lascivious Goth, and all the bitterest terms   110
That ever ear did hear to such effect,
And had you not by wondrous fortune come,
This vengeance on me had they executed.
Revenge it, as you love your mother's life,
Or be ye not henceforth called my children.

DEMETRIUS
This is a witness that I am thy son.
   Stab him [Bassianus].

CHIRON
And this for me, struck home to show my strength.

LAVINIA
Ay, come, Semiramis, nay, barbarous Tamora,   118
For no name fits thy nature but thy own.

TAMORA
Give me the poniard; you shall know, my boys,   120
Your mother's hand shall right your mother's wrong.

DEMETRIUS
Stay, madam, here is more belongs to her:

---

97 *fatal raven* (the raven was associated with death because it scavenged bat-
tlefields)   101 *urchins* hedgehogs, or goblins   110 *Goth* (pun on the prover-
bially lecherous "goat")   118 *Semiramis* (see II.1.22 n.)   120 *poniard* dagger

123   First thrash the corn, then after burn the straw.
124   This minion stood upon her chastity,
      Upon her nuptial vow, her loyalty,
126   And with that painted hope braves your mightiness;
      And shall she carry this unto her grave?
CHIRON
128   An if she do, I would I were an eunuch.
      Drag hence her husband to some secret hole,
130   And make his dead trunk pillow to our lust.
TAMORA
      But when ye have the honey we desire,
132   Let not this wasp outlive, us both to sting.
CHIRON
      I warrant you, madam, we will make that sure.
      Come, mistress, now perforce we will enjoy
135   That nice-preservèd honesty of yours.
LAVINIA
      O Tamora, thou bearest a woman's face –
TAMORA
      I will not hear her speak, away with her!
LAVINIA
      Sweet lords, entreat her hear me but a word.
DEMETRIUS
      Listen, fair madam: let it be your glory
140   To see her tears; but be your heart to them
      As unrelenting flint to drops of rain.
LAVINIA
142   When did the tiger's young ones teach the dam?
143   O, do not learn her wrath; she taught it thee;
      The milk thou suck'dst from her did turn to marble;
      Even at thy teat thou hadst thy tyranny.

---

123 *thrash* thresh, but also beat a person; *corn* grain   124 *minion* slut (also a low-class person); *stood upon* made much or boasted of   126 *painted* false (some editors emend to "quaint," meaning "delicate," with an obscene pun on the female genitals)   128 *An if* if   132 *outlive* survive   135 *nice-preservèd honesty* carefully guarded chastity   142 *dam* mother   143 *learn* teach

Yet every mother breeds not sons alike.
  [To Chiron]
Do thou entreat her show a woman's pity.

CHIRON

What, wouldst thou have me prove myself a bastard?

LAVINIA

'Tis true the raven doth not hatch a lark:
Yet have I heard – O, could I find it now! –   150
The lion, moved with pity, did endure
To have his princely paws pared all away.
Some say that ravens foster forlorn children   153
The whilst their own birds famish in their nests:
O, be to me, though thy hard heart say no,
Nothing so kind, but something pitiful.   156

TAMORA

I know not what it means, away with her!

LAVINIA

O, let me teach thee for my father's sake,
That gave thee life when well he might have slain thee,
Be not obdurate, open thy deaf ears.   *160*

TAMORA

Hadst thou in person ne'er offended me,
Even for his sake am I pitiless.
Remember, boys, I poured forth tears in vain
To save your brother from the sacrifice,
But fierce Andronicus would not relent.
Therefore away with her, and use her as you will;
The worse to her, the better loved of me.

LAVINIA

O Tamora, be called a gentle queen
And with thine own hands kill me in this place,
For 'tis not life that I have begged so long.   170
Poor I was slain when Bassianus died.

---

150 *find* discover, find to be true **153** *forlorn* abandoned **156** i.e., not so kind as the raven, yet showing some pity **170** *'tis not life . . . so long* I have been begging for pity, not for life

TAMORA

172   What begg'st thou then? fond woman, let me go.

LAVINIA

    'Tis present death I beg, and one thing more

174   That womanhood denies my tongue to tell.

    O, keep me from their worse than killing lust,

    And tumble me into some loathsome pit,

    Where never man's eye may behold my body.

    Do this, and be a charitable murderer.

TAMORA

179   So should I rob my sweet sons of their fee.

180   No, let them satisfice their lust on thee.

DEMETRIUS

    Away! for thou hast stayed us here too long.

LAVINIA

    No grace? no womanhood? Ah, beastly creature,

183   The blot and enemy to our general name!

184   Confusion fall –

CHIRON

    Nay then, I'll stop your mouth. Bring thou her husband.

    This is the hole where Aaron bid us hide him.

    [Demetrius throws the body of Bassianus into the pit;
    then exeunt Demetrius and Chiron, dragging off
    Lavinia.]

TAMORA

187   Farewell, my sons: see that you make her sure.

    Ne'er let my heart know merry cheer indeed

189   Till all the Andronici be made away.

190   Now will I hence to seek my lovely Moor

191   And let my spleenful sons this trull deflower.   *[Exit.]*

---

172 *fond* foolish   174 *denies* forbids   179 *fee* hunting dog's share of the captured game   183 *our general name* the name of woman   184 *Confusion* destruction   187 *sure* safe i.e., incapable of revenge   189 *made away* done away with   191 *spleenful* passionate; *trull* whore

Enter Aaron, with two of Titus' sons [Quintus and
Martius].

AARON
  Come on, my lords, the better foot before.
  Straight will I bring you to the loathsome pit
  Where I espied the panther fast asleep.

QUINTUS
  My sight is very dull, whate'er it bodes.   195

MARTIUS
  And mine, I promise you: were it not for shame,
  Well could I leave our sport to sleep awhile.
    [Falls into the pit.]

QUINTUS
  What, art thou fallen? What subtle hole is this,
  Whose mouth is covered with rude-growing briers,
  Upon whose leaves are drops of new-shed blood   *200*
  As fresh as morning dew distilled on flowers?
  A very fatal place it seems to me.   *202*
  Speak, brother, hast thou hurt thee with the fall?

MARTIUS
  O brother, with the dismallest object hurt
  That ever eye with sight made heart lament.

AARON
  Now will I fetch the king to find them here,
  That he thereby may have a likely guess
  How these were they that made away his brother. *Exit.*

MARTIUS
  Why dost not comfort me and help me out
  From this unhallowed and bloodstainèd hole?   *210*

QUINTUS
  I am surprisèd with an uncouth fear;   *211*
  A chilling sweat o'erruns my trembling joints;
  My heart suspects more than mine eye can see.

---

195 (lethargy was considered a bad omen)   **202** *fatal* ill-omened   **211** *un-couth* strange

MARTIUS

214   To prove thou hast a true-divining heart,
       Aaron and thou look down into this den
       And see a fearful sight of blood and death.

QUINTUS

       Aaron is gone, and my compassionate heart
       Will not permit mine eyes once to behold
219   The thing whereat it trembles by surmise.
220   O, tell me who it is, for ne'er till now
       Was I a child to fear I know not what.

MARTIUS

222   Lord Bassianus lies berayed in blood,
       All on a heap, like to a slaughterèd lamb,
       In this detested, dark, blood-drinking pit.

QUINTUS

       If it be dark, how dost thou know 'tis he?

MARTIUS

       Upon his bloody finger he doth wear
       A precious ring that lightens all this hole,
228   Which, like a taper in some monument,
       Doth shine upon the dead man's earthy cheeks,
230   And shows the ragged entrails of this pit.
231   So pale did shine the moon on Pyramus
       When he by night lay bathed in maiden blood.
       O brother, help me with thy fainting hand,
       If fear hath made thee faint, as me it hath,
235   Out of this fell devouring receptacle,
236   As hateful as Cocytus' misty mouth.

QUINTUS

       Reach me thy hand, that I may help thee out,
238   Or, wanting strength to do thee so much good,
       I may be plucked into the swallowing womb

---

214 *true-divining* prophetic   219 *by surmise* to imagine   222 *berayed* befouled   228 *taper* candle; *monument* tomb   230 *ragged entrails* rough interior   231 *Pyramus* the lover of Thisbe, who killed himself, thinking her dead 235 *fell* savage   236 *Cocytus* a river in Hades   238 *wanting* lacking

Of this deep pit, poor Bassianus' grave.   240
I have no strength to pluck thee to the brink.
MARTIUS
Nor I no strength to climb without thy help.
QUINTUS
Thy hand once more; I will not loose again
Till thou art here aloft, or I below.
Thou canst not come to me: I come to thee. *[Falls in.]*
    Enter the Emperor and Aaron the Moor.
SATURNINUS
Along with me: I'll see what hole is here,
And what he is that now is leaped into it.
Say, who art thou that lately didst descend
Into this gaping hollow of the earth?
MARTIUS
The unhappy sons of old Andronicus,   250
Brought hither in a most unlucky hour
To find thy brother Bassianus dead.
SATURNINUS
My brother dead? I know thou dost but jest.
He and his lady both are at the lodge
Upon the north side of this pleasant chase;
'Tis not an hour since I left them there.
MARTIUS
We know not where you left them all alive;
But, out alas! here have we found him dead.
    Enter Tamora, Andronicus, and Lucius.
TAMORA
Where is my lord the king?
SATURNINUS
Here, Tamora; though grieved with killing grief.   260
TAMORA
Where is thy brother Bassianus?
SATURNINUS
Now to the bottom dost thou search my wound: 262

----

262 *search* probe

Poor Bassianus here lies murderèd.

TAMORA

Then all too late I bring this fatal writ,

265   The complot of this timeless tragedy,

266   And wonder greatly that man's face can fold

In pleasing smiles such murderous tyranny.

She giveth Saturnine a letter.

SATURNINUS   *Reads the letter.*

268   "An if we miss to meet him handsomely,

Sweet huntsman – Bassianus 'tis we mean –

270   Do thou so much as dig the grave for him.

Thou know'st our meaning: look for thy reward

Among the nettles at the elder tree

Which overshades the mouth of that same pit

Where we decreed to bury Bassianus.

Do this, and purchase us thy lasting friends."

O Tamora, was ever heard the like?

This is the pit, and this the elder tree.

Look, sirs, if you can find the huntsman out

279   That should have murdered Bassianus here.

AARON

280   My gracious lord, here is the bag of gold.

SATURNINUS   *[To Titus]*

281   Two of thy whelps, fell curs of bloody kind,

Have here bereft my brother of his life.

Sirs, drag them from the pit unto the prison.

There let them bide until we have devised

Some never-heard-of torturing pain for them.

TAMORA

What, are they in this pit? O wondrous thing!

How easily murder is discoverèd!

TITUS

High emperor, upon my feeble knee

289   I beg this boon, with tears not lightly shed,

---

265 *complot* plot; *timeless* untimely   266 *fold* conceal   268 *handsomely* conveniently   279 *should* was to   281 *fell* cruel; *kind* nature   289 *boon* favor

That this fell fault of my accursèd sons,   *290*
Accursèd if the fault be proved in them –
SATURNINUS
  If it be proved? You see it is apparent.
  Who found this letter? Tamora, was it you?
TAMORA
  Andronicus himself did take it up.
TITUS
  I did, my lord, yet let me be their bail;
  For by my father's reverend tomb I vow
  They shall be ready at your highness' will
  To answer their suspicion with their lives.   *298*
SATURNINUS
  Thou shalt not bail them: see thou follow me.
  Some bring the murdered body, some the murderers.   *300*
  Let them not speak a word; the guilt is plain;
  For, by my soul, were there worse end than death,
  That end upon them should be executed.
TAMORA
  Andronicus, I will entreat the king;
  Fear not thy sons, they shall do well enough.   *305*
TITUS
  Come, Lucius, come, stay not to talk with them.
                                         [Exeunt.]

                        *

∾ **II.4** *Enter the Empress' sons [Demetrius and Chiron],
    with Lavinia, her hands cut off, and her tongue cut
    out, and ravished.*

DEMETRIUS
  So, now go tell, an if thy tongue can speak,
  Who 'twas that cut thy tongue and ravished thee.

---

298 *their suspicion* suspicion of them   **305** *Fear not* fear not for
II.4 The forest

CHIRON

3   Write down thy mind, bewray thy meaning so,
     An if thy stumps will let thee play the scribe.

DEMETRIUS

5   See how with signs and tokens she can scrawl.

CHIRON

6   Go home, call for sweet water, wash thy hands.

DEMETRIUS

     She hath no tongue to call, nor hands to wash,
     And so let's leave her to her silent walks.

CHIRON

9   An 'twere my cause, I should go hang myself.

DEMETRIUS

10   If thou hadst hands to help thee knit the cord.

                         Exeunt [Demetrius and Chiron].
          Enter Marcus, from hunting.

MARCUS

     Who is this? my niece, that flies away so fast!

12   Cousin, a word: where is your husband?

13   If I do dream, would all my wealth would wake me!
     If I do wake, some planet strike me down,
     That I may slumber an eternal sleep!
     Speak, gentle niece, what stern ungentle hand
     Hath lopped and hewed and made thy body bare
     Of her two branches, those sweet ornaments
     Whose circling shadows kings have sought to sleep in,

20   And might not gain so great a happiness
     As half thy love? Why dost not speak to me?
     Alas, a crimson river of warm blood,
     Like to a bubbling fountain stirred with wind,
     Doth rise and fall between thy rosèd lips,
     Coming and going with thy honey breath.

---

3 *bewray* reveal   5 *scrawl* gesticulate (with the sense of "scribble")   6 *sweet* perfumed   9 *cause* case   12 *Cousin* kinswoman (used of a relative more distant than brother or sister)   13 *would all my wealth would wake me* I would give all I have to awaken   20–21 *And might not gain . . . half thy love* and could never find joy as great as half your love

But sure some Tereus hath deflowered thee,   26
And, lest thou shouldst detect him, cut thy tongue.   27
Ah, now thou turn'st away thy face for shame,
And, notwithstanding all this loss of blood,
As from a conduit with three issuing spouts,   30
Yet do thy cheeks look red as Titan's face   31
Blushing to be encountered with a cloud.
Shall I speak for thee? Shall I say 'tis so?
O that I knew thy heart, and knew the beast,
That I might rail at him to ease my mind!
Sorrow concealèd, like an oven stopped,
Doth burn the heart to cinders where it is.
Fair Philomel, why she but lost her tongue,   38
And in a tedious sampler sewed her mind: 39
But, lovely niece, that mean is cut from thee;   40
A craftier Tereus, cousin, hast thou met,
And he hath cut those pretty fingers off
That could have better sewed than Philomel.
O, had the monster seen those lily hands
Tremble like aspen leaves upon a lute
And make the silken strings delight to kiss them,
He would not then have touched them for his life.
Or had he heard the heavenly harmony
Which that sweet tongue hath made,
He would have dropped his knife, and fell asleep,   50
As Cerberus at the Thracian poet's feet.   51
Come, let us go and make thy father blind,
For such a sight will blind a father's eye.
One hour's storm will drown the fragrant meads;   54
What will whole months of tears thy father's eyes?
Do not draw back, for we will mourn with thee:
O, could our mourning ease thy misery!   *Exeunt.*

---

26 *Tereus* legendary rapist (see II.3.43 n.)   27 *detect* expose   30 *conduit* fountain   31 *Titan* the sun god (see I.1.229 n.)   38 *Philomel* legendary rape victim (see II.3.43 n.)   39 *tedious sampler* laboriously executed embroidery   51 *Cerberus* three-headed dog that guarded the entrance to Hades; *Thracian poet* Orpheus, whose music lulled Cerberus asleep   54 *meads* meadows

*

❧ **III.1** *Enter the Judges and Senators, with Titus' two
sons [Martius and Quintus], bound, passing on the
stage to the place of execution, and Titus going before,
pleading.*

TITUS
 Hear me, grave fathers! noble tribunes, stay,
 For pity of mine age, whose youth was spent
 In dangerous wars whilst you securely slept.
 For all my blood in Rome's great quarrel shed,
 For all the frosty nights that I have watched,
 And for these bitter tears which now you see
 Filling the agèd wrinkles in my cheeks,
 Be pitiful to my condemnèd sons,
 Whose souls are not corrupted as 'tis thought.
10 For two and twenty sons I never wept,
 Because they died in honor's lofty bed.
  Andronicus lieth down, and the Judges pass by him.
 For these, tribunes, in the dust I write
13 My heart's deep languor and my soul's sad tears.
14 Let my tears staunch the earth's dry appetite;
 My sons' sweet blood will make it shame and blush.
 O earth, I will befriend thee more with rain
17 That shall distill from these two ancient urns
 Than youthful April shall with all his showers.
19 In summer's drought I'll drop upon thee still,
20 In winter with warm tears I'll melt the snow,
 And keep eternal springtime on thy face,
22 So thou refuse to drink my dear sons' blood.
  Enter Lucius, with his weapon drawn.
 O reverend tribunes! O gentle agèd men!

III.1 A street in Rome 13 *languor* grief 14 *staunch* satisfy 17 *urns* i.e., his
eyes (the early texts print "ruins") 19 *still* incessantly 22 *So* provided that

Unbind my sons, reverse the doom of death;   24
And let me say, that never wept before,
My tears are now prevailing orators!
LUCIUS
O noble father, you lament in vain,
The tribunes hear you not; no man is by,
And you recount your sorrows to a stone.
TITUS
Ah, Lucius, for thy brothers let me plead.   30
Grave tribunes, once more I entreat of you –
LUCIUS
My gracious lord, no tribune hears you speak.
TITUS
Why, 'tis no matter, man: if they did hear,
They would not mark me; or if they did mark,
They would not pity me; yet plead I must,
And bootless unto them.   36
Therefore I tell my sorrows to the stones,
Who, though they cannot answer my distress,
Yet in some sort they are better than the tribunes,
For that they will not intercept my tale.   40
When I do weep, they humbly at my feet
Receive my tears and seem to weep with me,
And were they but attirèd in grave weeds,   43
Rome could afford no tribunes like to these.
A stone is soft as wax, tribunes more hard than stones:
A stone is silent and offendeth not,
And tribunes with their tongues doom men to death.
    [Rises.]
But wherefore stand'st thou with thy weapon drawn?
LUCIUS
To rescue my two brothers from their death,
For which attempt the judges have pronounced   50

---

24 *doom* sentence **36** *And bootless unto them* useless to plead with them
(some editors consider the line an authorial false start printed erroneously,
and therefore omit it) **40** *intercept* interrupt **43** *grave weeds* sober dress

My everlasting doom of banishment.

TITUS

    O happy man! they have befriended thee.
    Why, foolish Lucius, dost thou not perceive
    That Rome is but a wilderness of tigers?
    Tigers must prey, and Rome affords no prey
    But me and mine: how happy art thou then
    From these devourers to be banishèd!
    But who comes with our brother Marcus here?
      Enter Marcus with Lavinia.

MARCUS

    Titus, prepare thy agèd eyes to weep,
60   Or if not so, thy noble heart to break!
61   I bring consuming sorrow to thine age.

TITUS

    Will it consume me? let me see it then.

MARCUS

    This was thy daughter.

TITUS   Why, Marcus, so she is.

LUCIUS

64   Ay me, this object kills me!

TITUS

    Faint-hearted boy, arise and look upon her.
    Speak, Lavinia, what accursèd hand
    Hath made thee handless in thy father's sight?
    What fool hath added water to the sea
69   Or brought a faggot to bright-burning Troy?
70   My grief was at the height before thou cam'st,
71   And now like Nilus it disdaineth bounds.
    Give me a sword: I'll chop off my hands too,
    For they have fought for Rome, and all in vain;
    And they have nursed this woe in feeding life;
    In bootless prayer have they been held up,
    And they have served me to effectless use.

---

61 *consuming* destroying **64** *Ay me* alas; *object* spectacle **69** *faggot* bundle of firewood **71** *Nilus* the Nile

Now all the service I require of them
Is that the one will help to cut the other.
'Tis well, Lavinia, that thou hast no hands,
For hands to do Rome service is but vain. 80

LUCIUS
Speak, gentle sister, who hath martyred thee? 81

MARCUS
O, that delightful engine of her thoughts 82
That blabbed them with such pleasing eloquence
Is torn from forth that pretty hollow cage,
Where like a sweet melodious bird it sung
Sweet varied notes, enchanting every ear!

LUCIUS
O, say thou for her, who hath done this deed?

MARCUS
O, thus I found her straying in the park,
Seeking to hide herself, as doth the deer
That hath received some unrecuring wound. 90

TITUS
It was my dear, and he that wounded her
Hath hurt me more than had he killed me dead;
For now I stand as one upon a rock,
Environed with a wilderness of sea,
Who marks the waxing tide grow wave by wave,
Expecting ever when some envious surge 96
Will in his brinish bowels swallow him.
This way to death my wretched sons are gone;
Here stands my other son, a banished man,
And here my brother, weeping at my woes: 100
But that which gives my soul the greatest spurn 101
Is dear Lavinia, dearer than my soul.
Had I but seen thy picture in this plight,
It would have madded me: what shall I do

---

81 *martyred* mutilated, tortured **82** *engine* instrument **90** *unrecuring* incurable **96** *envious* malignant **101** *spurn* contemptuous kick

105   Now I behold thy lively body so?
        Thou hast no hands to wipe away thy tears,
        Nor tongue to tell me who hath martyred thee.
        Thy husband he is dead, and for his death
109   Thy brothers are condemned, and dead by this.
110   Look, Marcus! ah, son Lucius, look on her!
        When I did name her brothers, then fresh tears
112   Stood on her cheeks, as doth the honey dew
        Upon a gathered lily almost withered.

MARCUS
        Perchance she weeps because they killed her husband,
        Perchance because she knows them innocent.

TITUS
        If they did kill thy husband, then be joyful,
        Because the law hath ta'en revenge on them.
        No, no, they would not do so foul a deed;
119   Witness the sorrow that their sister makes.
120   Gentle Lavinia, let me kiss thy lips,
121   Or make some sign how I may do thee ease.
        Shall thy good uncle and thy brother Lucius
        And thou and I sit round about some fountain,
        Looking all downwards to behold our cheeks
        How they are stained, like meadows yet not dry
        With miry slime left on them by a flood?
        And in the fountain shall we gaze so long
128   Till the fresh taste be taken from that clearness,
        And made a brine pit with our bitter tears?
130   Or shall we cut away our hands like thine?
131   Or shall we bite our tongues, and in dumb shows
        Pass the remainder of our hateful days?
        What shall we do? let us that have our tongues
        Plot some device of further misery,
        To make us wondered at in time to come.

---

105 *lively* living   109 *by this* by now   112 *honey dew* sweet dewlike liquid
119 *makes* expresses (through tears or gestures)   121 *do thee ease* relieve you
128 *clearness* i.e., clear fountain   131 *dumb shows* mime

LUCIUS
    Sweet father, cease your tears; for at your grief
    See how my wretched sister sobs and weeps.

MARCUS
    Patience, dear niece. Good Titus, dry thine eyes.
    [Gives him a handkerchief.]

TITUS
    Ah, Marcus, Marcus! brother, well I wot
    Thy napkin cannot drink a tear of mine,   140
    For thou, poor man, hast drowned it with thine own.   141

LUCIUS
    Ah, my Lavinia, I will wipe thy cheeks.

TITUS
    Mark, Marcus, mark! I understand her signs:
    Had she a tongue to speak, now would she say
    That to her brother which I said to thee.
    His napkin, with his true tears all bewet,
    Can do no service on her sorrowful cheeks.
    O, what a sympathy of woe is this: 148
    As far from help as Limbo is from bliss!   149
      Enter Aaron the Moor, alone.

AARON
    Titus Andronicus, my lord the emperor   150
    Sends thee this word, that, if thou love thy sons,
    Let Marcus, Lucius, or thyself, old Titus,
    Or any one of you, chop off your hand
    And send it to the king: he for the same
    Will send thee hither both thy sons alive,
    And that shall be the ransom for their fault.

TITUS
    O gracious emperor! O gentle Aaron!
    Did ever raven sing so like a lark
    That gives sweet tidings of the sun's uprise?
    With all my heart I'll send the emperor my hand.   160

---

140 *napkin* handkerchief **141** *drowned* soaked **148** *sympathy* harmony
149 *Limbo* region bordering hell, eternal home of the unbaptized

Good Aaron, wilt thou help to chop it off?
LUCIUS
　　Stay, father, for that noble hand of thine,
　　That hath thrown down so many enemies,
　　Shall not be sent: my hand will serve the turn,
　　My youth can better spare my blood than you,
　　And therefore mine shall save my brothers' lives.
MARCUS
　　Which of your hands hath not defended Rome
　　And reared aloft the bloody battle-ax,
169　Writing destruction on the enemy's casque?
170　O, none of both but are of high desert:
　　My hand hath been but idle; let it serve
　　To ransom my two nephews from their death;
　　Then have I kept it to a worthy end.
AARON
　　Nay, come, agree whose hand shall go along,
　　For fear they die before their pardon come.
MARCUS
　　My hand shall go.
LUCIUS　　　　　　By heaven, it shall not go!
TITUS
　　Sirs, strive no more. Such withered herbs as these
178　Are meet for plucking up, and therefore mine.
LUCIUS
　　Sweet father, if I shall be thought thy son,
180　Let me redeem my brothers both from death.
MARCUS
　　And for our father's sake and mother's care,
　　Now let me show a brother's love to thee.
TITUS
183　Agree between you; I will spare my hand.

---

169 *casque* helmet (*castle* in early texts)　**170** *none of both . . . desert* both of
you are worthy　**178** *meet* fit　**183** *spare* (in one sense, "save"; in another,
"do without")

LUCIUS
    Then I'll go fetch an ax.
MARCUS
    But I will use the ax.   *Exeunt [Lucius and Marcus].*
TITUS
    Come hither, Aaron. I'll deceive them both:
    Lend me thy hand, and I will give thee mine.
AARON   *[Aside]*
    If that be called deceit, I will be honest,
    And never whilst I live deceive men so:
    But I'll deceive you in another sort,   *190*
    And that you'll say ere half an hour pass.   191
        He cuts off Titus' hand.
        Enter Lucius and Marcus again.
TITUS
    Now stay your strife; what shall be is dispatched.
    Good Aaron, give his majesty my hand:
    Tell him it was a hand that warded him   194
    From thousand dangers; bid him bury it;
    More hath it merited, that let it have.
    As for my sons, say I account of them
    As jewels purchased at an easy price,
    And yet dear too, because I bought mine own.   199
AARON
    I go, Andronicus, and for thy hand   *200*
    Look by and by to have thy sons with thee.   201
        [Aside]
    Their heads, I mean. O, how this villainy
    Doth fat me with the very thoughts of it!   203
    Let fools do good, and fair men call for grace,
    Aaron will have his soul black like his face.   *Exit.*
TITUS
    O, here I lift this one hand up to heaven,
    And bow this feeble ruin to the earth.

---

191 *that you'll say* you'll agree that I did so   194 *warded* protected   199
dear expensive   201 *Look* expect   203 *fat* delight (literally, "nourish")

If any power pities wretched tears,
To that I call!
  [To Lavinia]
                    What, wouldst thou kneel with me?
210 Do then, dear heart, for heaven shall hear our prayers,
211 Or with our sighs we'll breathe the welkin dim
     And stain the sun with fog, as sometime clouds
213 When they do hug him in their melting bosoms.
MARCUS
     O brother, speak with possibility,
     And do not break into these deep extremes.
TITUS
     Is not my sorrow deep, having no bottom?
217 Then be my passions bottomless with them!
MARCUS
     But yet let reason govern thy lament.
TITUS
     If there were reason for these miseries,
220 Then into limits could I bind my woes:
     When heaven doth weep, doth not the earth o'erflow?
     If the winds rage, doth not the sea wax mad,
     Threatening the welkin with his big-swollen face?
224 And wilt thou have a reason for this coil?
     I am the sea; hark how her sighs doth blow!
     She is the weeping welkin, I the earth:
     Then must my sea be movèd with her sighs,
     Then must my earth with her continual tears
     Become a deluge, overflowed and drowned,
230 For why my bowels cannot hide her woes,
     But like a drunkard must I vomit them.
     Then give me leave; for losers will have leave

---

211 *breathe . . . dim* cloud the heavens (*welkin*) with our breath   213 *melt-ing* raining   217 *passions* outbursts   220 *bind* confine   224 *coil* disturbance
230 *For why* because; *bowels* i.e., the interior of the body, the heart (the bow-els were associated with compassion), but also the bowels of the earth (l. 228), as in a volcanic eruption; *her* older form of the possessive "their"

To ease their stomachs with their bitter tongues.   233
Enter a Messenger, with two heads and a hand.

MESSENGER
Worthy Andronicus, ill art thou repaid
For that good hand thou sent'st the emperor.
Here are the heads of thy two noble sons,
And here's thy hand, in scorn to thee sent back,
Thy grief their sports, thy resolution mocked,
That woe is me to think upon thy woes   239
More than remembrance of my father's death.   *Exit.* 240

MARCUS
Now let hot Etna cool in Sicily,   241
And be my heart an ever-burning hell!
These miseries are more than may be borne.
To weep with them that weep doth ease some deal;   244
But sorrow flouted at is double death.   245

LUCIUS
Ah, that this sight should make so deep a wound,
And yet detested life not shrink thereat;   247
That ever death should let life bear his name   248
Where life hath no more interest but to breathe!   249
[Lavinia kisses the two heads.]

MARCUS
Alas, poor heart, that kiss is comfortless   250
As frozen water to a starvèd snake.   251

TITUS
When will this fearful slumber have an end?   252

MARCUS
Now farewell, flattery; die, Andronicus;   253

---

233 *ease their stomachs* relieve their feelings   239 *That* so that   241 *hot Etna* (Sicilian volcano)   244 *some deal* somewhat   245 *flouted* mocked   247 *shrink* retreat, fail   248 *bear his name* i.e., still be called "life"   249 *interest* entitlement, right (legal term); **s.d.** *[Lavinia kisses the two heads.]* This stage direction was convincingly proposed by Jonathan Bate in his 1995 Arden edition; most editors direct her to kiss Titus.   251 *starvèd* numbed by cold   252 *fearful slumber* i.e., nightmare   253 *flattery* delusion (that the nightmare will end)

Thou dost not slumber: see thy two sons' heads,
Thy warlike hand, thy mangled daughter here,
256 Thy other banished son with this dear sight
Struck pale and bloodless, and thy brother, I,
Even like a stony image, cold and numb.
259 Ah, now no more will I control thy griefs:
260 Rend off thy silver hair, thy other hand
Gnawing with thy teeth; and be this dismal sight
The closing up of our most wretched eyes.
Now is a time to storm; why art thou still?

TITUS Ha, ha, ha!

MARCUS
Why dost thou laugh? it fits not with this hour.

TITUS
Why, I have not another tear to shed;
Besides, this sorrow is an enemy,
And would usurp upon my watery eyes
And make them blind with tributary tears.
270 Then which way shall I find Revenge's cave?
For these two heads do seem to speak to me,
And threat me I shall never come to bliss
Till all these mischiefs be returned again
Even in their throats that hath committed them.
Come, let me see what task I have to do.
276 You heavy people, circle me about,
That I may turn me to each one of you
And swear unto my soul to right your wrongs.
The vow is made. Come, brother, take a head;
280 And in this hand the other will I bear.
281 And, Lavinia, thou shalt be employed [. . . .]
Bear thou my hand, sweet wench, between thy teeth.

---

256 *dear* grievous 259 *control* restrain 276 *heavy* mournful 281 *employed [. . . .]* (A textual problem: Q reads *employed in these arms*; F *employed in these things*. It may be that someone preparing the manuscript for Q inserted "arms" as a less grotesque substitute for "teeth" in the following line, and that the insertion was mistakenly picked up by the compositor and printed here; the original reading could have been "employed in this.")

As for thee, boy, go get thee from my sight,
Thou art an exile, and thou must not stay.
Hie to the Goths and raise an army there;
And if ye love me, as I think you do,
Let's kiss and part, for we have much to do.
                                    Exeunt [all except Lucius].

LUCIUS
Farewell, Andronicus, my noble father,
The woefull'st man that ever lived in Rome.
Farewell, proud Rome, till Lucius come again!   290
He loves his pledges dearer than his life.   291
Farewell, Lavinia, my noble sister.
O, would thou wert as thou tofore hast been!   293
But now nor Lucius nor Lavinia lives
But in oblivion and hateful griefs.
If Lucius live, he will requite your wrongs
And make proud Saturnine and his empress
Beg at the gates like Tarquin and his queen.   298
Now will I to the Goths and raise a power,   299
To be revenged on Rome and Saturnine.   *Exit Lucius.* 300

                          *

∾ **III.2** *A banquet. Enter Andronicus, Marcus, Lavinia,
    and the Boy [Young Lucius].*

TITUS
So, so, now sit; and look you eat no more
Than will preserve just so much strength in us
As will revenge these bitter woes of ours.
Marcus, unknit that sorrow-wreathen knot: 4
Thy niece and I, poor creatures, want our hands,
And cannot passionate our tenfold grief   6

---

291 *pledges* vows (but perhaps also his family members, who guarantee his
return)   293 *tofore* formerly   298 *Tarquin* (Roman king, deposed when his
son, also named Tarquin, raped Lucrece)   299 *power* army
    III.2 Titus's house (the quartos lack this scene; it appears only in F)   4
knot i.e., folded arms (signifying sorrow)   6 *passionate* express with passion

With folded arms. This poor right hand of mine
Is left to tyrannize upon my breast;
Who, when my heart, all mad with misery,
10 Beats in this hollow prison of my flesh,
Then thus I thump it down.
      [To Lavinia]
12 Thou map of woe, that thus dost talk in signs,
When thy poor heart beats with outrageous beating,
Thou canst not strike it thus to make it still.
15 Wound it with sighing, girl, kill it with groans;
Or get some little knife between thy teeth
And just against thy heart make thou a hole,
That all the tears that thy poor eyes let fall
19 May run into that sink, and soaking in,
20 Drown the lamenting fool in sea-salt tears.

MARCUS
Fie, brother, fie! teach her not thus to lay
Such violent hands upon her tender life.

TITUS
How now! has sorrow made thee dote already?
Why, Marcus, no man should be mad but I.
What violent hands can she lay on her life?
Ah, wherefore dost thou urge the name of hands,
27 To bid Aeneas tell the tale twice o'er,
How Troy was burnt and he made miserable?
O, handle not the theme, to talk of hands,
30 Lest we remember still that we have none.
31 Fie, fie, how franticly I square my talk,
As if we should forget we had no hands
If Marcus did not name the word of hands!
Come, let's fall to; and, gentle girl, eat this.

---

12 *map* pattern 15 (sighs and groans were thought to shorten life by weakening the heart) 19 *sink* receptacle 20 *fool* (here, as often, a term of affection) 27 *Aeneas* (Virgil's hero laments that the retelling of his story rekindles his misery, in *Aeneid* II.2) 31 *square* regulate

Here is no drink! hark, Marcus, what she says.
I can interpret all her martyred signs:
She says she drinks no other drink but tears,
Brewed with her sorrow, meshed upon her cheeks.   38
Speechless complainer, I will learn thy thought.
In thy dumb action will I be as perfect   40
As begging hermits in their holy prayers.
Thou shalt not sigh, nor hold thy stumps to heaven,
Nor wink, nor nod, nor kneel, nor make a sign,   43
But I of these will wrest an alphabet
And by still practice learn to know thy meaning.   45

BOY

Good grandsire, leave these bitter deep laments.
Make my aunt merry with some pleasing tale.

MARCUS

Alas, the tender boy, in passion moved,
Doth weep to see his grandsire's heaviness.

TITUS

Peace, tender sapling, thou art made of tears,   50
And tears will quickly melt thy life away.
  Marcus strikes the dish with a knife.
What dost thou strike at, Marcus, with thy knife?

MARCUS

At that that I have killed, my lord – a fly.

TITUS

Out on thee, murderer! Thou kill'st my heart;
Mine eyes are cloyed with view of tyranny.   55
A deed of death done on the innocent
Becomes not Titus' brother. Get thee gone!
I see thou art not for my company.

MARCUS

Alas, my lord, I have but killed a fly.

---

38 *meshed* mashed (a brewing term) **40–41** *as perfect / As begging hermits* as skillful a reader as I would be of the gestures of praying hermits **43** *wink* blink **45** *still* constant **55** *cloyed* full to the point of nausea

TITUS

60   "But"? How if that fly had a father and mother?
How would he hang his slender gilded wings
62   And buzz lamenting doings in the air!
Poor harmless fly,
That, with his pretty buzzing melody,
Came here to make us merry, and thou hast killed him.

MARCUS

66   Pardon me, sir; it was a black ill-favored fly,
Like to the empress' Moor; therefore I killed him.

TITUS

O, O, O!

69   Then pardon me for reprehending thee,
70   For thou hast done a charitable deed.
71   Give me thy knife, I will insult on him,
72   Flattering myself as if it were the Moor
Come hither purposely to poison me.
               [Striking at the fly]
There's for thyself, and that's for Tamora.

75   Ah, sirrah!
Yet, I think, we are not brought so low
But that between us we can kill a fly
That comes in likeness of a coal-black Moor.

MARCUS

Alas, poor man! Grief has so wrought on him
80   He takes false shadows for true substances.

TITUS

81   Come, take away. Lavinia, go with me.
82   I'll to thy closet and go read with thee
83   Sad stories chancèd in the times of old.
Come, boy, and go with me. Thy sight is young,

---

60 *father and mother?* (some editors emend to *father, brother?*)   **62** *lamenting doings* lamentations (*doings* is perhaps an error for *dirges*)   **66** *ill-favored* ugly **69** *reprehending* correcting   **71** *insult on* triumph over   **72** *Flattering myself as if* deluding myself, pretending   **75** *sirrah* (contemptuous term of address to inferiors)   **81** *take away* clear the table   **82** *closet* private chamber   **83** *chancèd* that happened

And thou shalt read when mine begin to dazzle.   85

[Exeunt.]

*

∾ **IV.1** *Enter Lucius' son and Lavinia running after*
him, and the boy flies from her with his books under
his arm. Enter Titus and Marcus.

BOY
  Help, grandsire, help! My aunt Lavinia
  Follows me everywhere, I know not why.
  Good uncle Marcus, see how swift she comes:
  Alas, sweet aunt, I know not what you mean.
MARCUS
  Stand by me, Lucius; do not fear thine aunt.
TITUS
  She loves thee, boy, too well to do thee harm.
BOY
  Ay, when my father was in Rome she did.
MARCUS
  What means my niece Lavinia by these signs?
TITUS
  Fear her not, Lucius. Somewhat doth she mean.
MARCUS
  See, Lucius, see, how much she makes of thee: 10
  Somewhither would she have thee go with her.
  Ah, boy, Cornelia never with more care   12
  Read to her sons than she hath read to thee
  Sweet poetry and Tully's *Orator.*   14
  Canst thou not guess wherefore she plies thee thus?   15
BOY
  My lord, I know not, I, nor can I guess,

---

85 *mine begin to dazzle* my eyes become blurry
  IV.1 The garden of Titus's house   **10–15** *See, Lucius . . . thus* (the early
texts mistakenly assign this speech to Titus)   **12** *Cornelia* (mother of the
Gracchi, famous Roman tribunes)   **14** *Tully's* Orator (Cicero's *De Oratore* or
his *ad. M. Brutum Orator*)   **15** *plies* solicits, pesters

Unless some fit or frenzy do possess her,
For I have heard my grandsire say full oft,
Extremity of griefs would make men mad,
20 And I have read that Hecuba of Troy
Ran mad for sorrow. That made me to fear,
Although, my lord, I know my noble aunt
Loves me as dear as e'er my mother did,
24 And would not, but in fury, fright my youth,
Which made me down to throw my books, and fly,
Causeless, perhaps; but pardon me, sweet aunt,
And, madam, if my uncle Marcus go,
28 I will most willingly attend your ladyship.

MARCUS
Lucius, I will.
*[Lavinia turns over with her stumps the books which
Lucius has let fall.]*

TITUS
30 How now, Lavinia? Marcus, what means this?
Some book there is that she desires to see.
Which is it, girl, of these? Open them, boy.
[To Lavinia]
33 But thou art deeper read and better skilled:
Come and take choice of all my library,
And so beguile thy sorrow, till the heavens
Reveal the damned contriver of this deed.
37 Why lifts she up her arms in sequence thus?

MARCUS
I think she means that there were more than one
39 Confederate in the fact. Ay, more there was,
40 Or else to heaven she heaves them for revenge.

TITUS
41 Lucius, what book is that she tosseth so?

---

20 *Hecuba* (Trojan Queen, wife of Priam, who went mad when the Greeks
invaded Troy)   24 *but in fury* except in madness   28 *attend* accompany   33
better skilled more experienced (i.e., better than the boy at difficult reading)
37 *in sequence* one after the other   39 *fact* crime   41 *tosseth* fumbles with (as
she turns the leaves)

BOY
  Grandsire, 'tis Ovid's *Metamorphosis*.   42
  My mother gave it me.
MARCUS   For love of her that's gone
  Perhaps she culled it from among the rest.   44
TITUS
  Soft, so busily she turns the leaves!
  Help her: what would she find? Lavinia, shall I read?   46
  This is the tragic tale of Philomel   47
  And treats of Tereus' treason and his rape;
  And rape, I fear, was root of thine annoy.   49
MARCUS
  See, brother, see, note how she quotes the leaves.   50
TITUS
  Lavinia, wert thou thus surprised, sweet girl,
  Ravished and wronged as Philomela was,
  Forced in the ruthless, vast, and gloomy woods?   53
  See, see!
  Ay, such a place there is where we did hunt
  (O had we never, never hunted there!)
  Patterned by that the poet here describes,   57
  By nature made for murders and for rapes.
MARCUS
  O, why should nature build so foul a den,
  Unless the gods delight in tragedies?   60
TITUS
  Give signs, sweet girl, for here are none but friends,
  What Roman lord it was durst do the deed.
  Or slunk not Saturnine, as Tarquin erst,   63
  That left the camp to sin in Lucrece' bed?

---

42 *Ovid's* Metamorphosis (the spelling of Arthur Golding's 1565 translation of *Metamorphoses;* it was one of Shakespeare's favorite books) 44 *culled* picked 46 *Help her* (possibly a stage direction mistakenly printed as dialogue) 47–48 *Philomel . . . Tereus* (see II.3.43 n.) 49 *annoy* anguish 50 *quotes* scrutinizes 53 *vast* desolate 57 *Patterned by* according to the model 63 *erst* once

MARCUS
 Sit down, sweet niece: brother, sit down by me.
66 Apollo, Pallas, Jove, or Mercury,
 Inspire me, that I may this treason find.
 My lord, look here: look here, Lavinia!
  He writes his name with his staff, and guides it with
  feet and mouth.
69 This sandy plot is plain; guide, if thou canst,
70 This after me. I have writ my name
 Without the help of any hand at all.
72 Cursed be that heart that forced us to this shift!
 Write thou, good niece, and here display at last
74 What God will have discovered for revenge.
 Heaven guide thy pen to print thy sorrows plain,
 That we may know the traitors and the truth.
  She takes the staff in her mouth and guides it with her
  stumps and writes.
 O, do ye read, my lord, what she hath writ?
TITUS
78 *Stuprum. Chiron. Demetrius.*
MARCUS
 What, what! the lustful sons of Tamora
80 Performers of this heinous bloody deed?
TITUS
81 *Magni dominator poli,*
 Tam lentus audis scelera? tam lentus vides?
MARCUS
 O, calm thee, gentle lord, although I know
 There is enough written upon this earth
 To stir a mutiny in the mildest thoughts
86 And arm the minds of infants to exclaims.

---

66 *Apollo, Pallas, Jove, or Mercury* (ancient gods, all associated with wisdom
or intelligence) **69** *plain* level **72** *shift* means (as in "makeshift") **74** *discovered* revealed **78** *Stuprum* rape (the early texts mistakenly assign this line
to Marcus) **81–82** *Magni . . . vides* ruler of the great heavens, art thou so
slow to hear and to see crimes (Seneca, *Hippolytus*, II.671–72) **86** *exclaims*
outcries

My lord, kneel down with me; Lavinia, kneel;
And kneel, sweet boy, the Roman Hector's hope;   88
And swear with me, as with the woeful fere   89
And father of that chaste dishonored dame,   90
Lord Junius Brutus sware for Lucrece' rape,   91
That we will prosecute by good advice   92
Mortal revenge upon these traitorous Goths,
And see their blood or die with this reproach.

TITUS
'Tis sure enough, an you knew how,
But if you hunt these bear whelps, then beware:
The dam will wake, an if she wind ye once.   97
She's with the lion deeply still in league,   98
And lulls him whilst she playeth on her back,
And when he sleeps will she do what she list.   100
You are a young huntsman, Marcus; let alone.
And come, I will go get a leaf of brass,
And with a gad of steel will write these words,   103
And lay it by: the angry northern wind
Will blow these sands like Sibyl's leaves abroad,   105
And where's our lesson then? Boy, what say you?

BOY
I say, my lord, that if I were a man,
Their mother's bedchamber should not be safe
For these base bondmen to the yoke of Rome.

MARCUS
Ay, that's my boy! thy father hath full oft   110
For his ungrateful country done the like.

BOY
And, uncle, so will I, an if I live.

---

88 *the Roman Hector* i.e., Lucius, who, as leader of the army, has become the Roman counterpart of Hector of Troy   89 *fere* husband   91 *Junius Brutus* leader of the revolt against the Tarquins   92 *by good advice* after careful consideration   97 *an . . . ye* if she gets wind of you   98 *lion* i.e., Saturninus (the royal beast)   100 *list* likes   103 *gad* spike   105 *Sibyl's leaves* (the prophecies of the Sibyl were written on leaves which were often scattered by the wind)

TITUS

Come, go with me into mine armory:

114 Lucius, I'll fit thee, and withal my boy

Shall carry from me to the empress' sons

Presents that I intend to send them both.

Come, come; thou'lt do my message, wilt thou not?

BOY

Ay, with my dagger in their bosoms, grandsire.

TITUS

No, boy, not so. I'll teach thee another course.

120 Lavinia, come. Marcus, look to my house.

121 Lucius and I'll go brave it at the court.

122 Ay, marry, will we, sir, and we'll be waited on.

       Exeunt [Titus, Lavinia, and Young Lucius].

MARCUS

O heavens, can you hear a good man groan

124 And not relent, or not compassion him?

125 Marcus, attend him in his ecstasy,

That hath more scars of sorrow in his heart

Than foemen's marks upon his battered shield,

But yet so just that he will not revenge.

129 Revenge the heavens for old Andronicus!   *Exit.*

       *

❧ **IV.2** *Enter Aaron, Chiron, and Demetrius at one*
door, and at the other door Young Lucius and another,
with a bundle of weapons, and verses writ upon them.

CHIRON

Demetrius, here's the son of Lucius;

He hath some message to deliver us.

---

114 *fit* furnish 121 *brave it* act defiantly 122 *marry* (interjection of affir-
mation); *waited on* attended to 124 *compassion* have compassion for 125
ecstasy madness 129 *Revenge the heavens* let the heavens take vengeance
IV.2 Saturninus's palace

AARON
    Ay, some mad message from his mad grandfather.
BOY
    My lords, with all the humbleness I may,
    I greet your honors from Andronicus –
      [Aside]
    And pray the Roman gods confound you both.   6
DEMETRIUS
    Gramercy, lovely Lucius, what's the news?
BOY   *[Aside]*
    That you are both deciphered, that's the news,   8
    For villains marked with rape.
      [Aloud]   May it please you,
    My grandsire, well-advised, hath sent by me   10
    The goodliest weapons of his armory
    To gratify your honorable youth,
    The hope of Rome, for so he bid me say;
    And so I do, and with his gifts present
    Your lordships, that, whenever you have need,
    You may be armèd and appointed well.   16
    And so I leave you both – *[Aside]* like bloody villains.
                        Exit [with Attendant].
DEMETRIUS
    What's here? a scroll, and written round about?   18
    Let's see.
    Integer vitae scelerisque purus   20
    Non eget Mauri iaculis nec arcu.
CHIRON
    O, 'tis a verse in Horace; I know it well.
    I read it in the grammar long ago.   23

---

6 *confound* thwart, destroy **8** *deciphered* detected **16** *appointed* equipped
18 *round about* all over **20–21** *Integer . . . arcu* he who is of upright life and
free from crime does not need the javelins or bow of the Moor (Horace,
Odes, I, xxii, 1–2) **23** *grammar* book of Latin grammar with sample verses
(Lily's grammar, in wide use in early modern England, contains this passage)

AARON
    Ay, just; a verse in Horace; right, you have it.
      [Aside]
    Now what a thing it is to be an ass!
26   Here's no sound jest! the old man hath found their guilt,
    And sends them weapons wrapped about with lines
28   That wound, beyond their feeling, to the quick.
29   But were our witty empress well afoot,
30   She would applaud Andronicus' conceit.
    But let her rest in her unrest awhile. –
    And now, young lords, was't not a happy star
    Led us to Rome, strangers, and more than so,
    Captives, to be advancèd to this height?
    It did me good before the palace gate
    To brave the tribune in his brother's hearing.

DEMETRIUS
    But me more good to see so great a lord
38   Basely insinuate and send us gifts.

AARON
    Had he not reason, Lord Demetrius?
40   Did you not use his daughter very friendly?

DEMETRIUS
    I would we had a thousand Roman dames
42   At such a bay, by turn to serve our lust.

CHIRON
    A charitable wish and full of love!

AARON
    Here lacks but your mother for to say amen.

CHIRON
    And that would she for twenty thousand more.

DEMETRIUS
    Come, let us go and pray to all the gods

---

26 *no sound jest* (ironic: "what a good joke")   28 *quick* vital part, center   **29**
witty quick-witted; *well afoot* up and about   **30** *conceit* device   **38** *insinuate*
to ingratiate oneself with; i.e., worm his way into our favor   **42** *At . . . bay*
thus cornered (a hunting term)

For our belovèd mother in her pains.   47
AARON   *[Aside]*
Pray to the devils; the gods have given us over.
    Trumpets sound.
DEMETRIUS
Why do the emperor's trumpets flourish thus?
CHIRON
Belike for joy the emperor hath a son.   50
DEMETRIUS
Soft, who comes here?   51
    Enter Nurse, with a blackamoor Child.
NURSE   God morrow, lords.
O, tell me, did you see Aaron the Moor?
AARON
Well, more or less, or ne'er a whit at all,   53
Here Aaron is; and what with Aaron now?
NURSE
O gentle Aaron, we are all undone!
Now help, or woe betide thee evermore!
AARON
Why, what a caterwauling dost thou keep!   57
What dost thou wrap and fumble in thine arms?
NURSE
O, that which I would hide from heaven's eye –
Our empress' shame and stately Rome's disgrace!   60
She is delivered, lords, she is delivered.
AARON
To whom?
NURSE   I mean she is brought abed.
AARON
Well, God give her good rest! What hath he sent her?

---

47 *pains* (of childbirth)   50 *Belike* probably   51 **s.d.** *blackamoor* dark-
skinned; African   51 *God morrow* abbreviation of "God give you good morrow"   53 *more . . . all* (Aaron puns on his blackness, *more/Moor,* and its
opposite, *whit/white*); *ne'er a whit* not a bit   57 *caterwauling* howling; *keep*
keep up

NURSE

64   A devil.

AARON   Why, then she is the devil's dam:

65   A joyful issue!

NURSE

    A joyless, dismal, black, and sorrowful issue!

    Here is the babe, as loathsome as a toad

    Amongst the fair-faced breeders of our clime.

    The empress sends it thee, thy stamp, thy seal,

70   And bids thee christen it with thy dagger's point.

AARON

71   Zounds, ye whore! is black so base a hue?

72   Sweet blowse, you are a beauteous blossom, sure.

DEMETRIUS

    Villain, what hast thou done?

AARON

    That which thou canst not undo.

CHIRON

    Thou hast undone our mother.

AARON

76   Villain, I have done thy mother.

DEMETRIUS

    And therein, hellish dog, thou hast undone her.

78   Woe to her chance, and damned her loathèd choice!

    Accursed the offspring of so foul a fiend!

CHIRON

80   It shall not live.

AARON

    It shall not die.

NURSE

    Aaron, it must; the mother wills it so.

AARON

    What, must it, nurse? then let no man but I

---

64 *dam* mother 65 *issue* offspring, outcome 71 *Zounds* (an oath; a contraction of "by God's wounds") 72 *blowse* red-cheeked wench (spoken ironically to the child) 76 *done* had sexual intercourse with 78 *chance* luck

Do execution on my flesh and blood.

DEMETRIUS

I'll broach the tadpole on my rapier's point.   85
Nurse, give it me; my sword shall soon dispatch it.

AARON

Sooner this sword shall plow thy bowels up.
Stay, murderous villains! will you kill your brother?
Now by the burning tapers of the sky,
That shone so brightly when this boy was got,   90
He dies upon my scimitar's sharp point
That touches this my first-born son and heir!
I tell you, younglings, not Enceladus,   93
With all his threat'ning band of Typhon's brood,
Nor great Alcides, nor the god of war,   95
Shall seize this prey out of his father's hands.
What, what, ye sanguine, shallow-hearted boys!   97
Ye white-limed walls! ye alehouse painted signs!   98
Coal-black is better than another hue
In that it scorns to bear another hue;   100
For all the water in the ocean
Can never turn the swan's black legs to white,
Although she lave them hourly in the flood.   103
Tell the empress from me I am of age
To keep mine own, excuse it how she can.

DEMETRIUS

Wilt thou betray thy noble mistress thus?

AARON

My mistress is my mistress; this myself,
The vigor and the picture of my youth.
This before all the world do I prefer,
This maugre all the world will I keep safe,   110

---

85 *broach* stick, stab   93 *Enceladus* (one of the legendary Titans, sons of Typhon, who fought the Olympians)   95 *Alcides* Hercules   97 *sanguine* red-
cheeked   98 *white-limed walls* hypocrites, "whited sepulchers" (Matthew
23:27); *alehouse painted signs* pictures of, not real men   100 *scorns to bear
another hue* (Aaron considers black superior to other colors because black
cloth could not be dyed)   103 *lave* wash   110 *maugre* in spite of

111 Or some of you shall smoke for it in Rome!
DEMETRIUS
By this our mother is for ever shamed.
CHIRON
Rome will despise her for this foul escape.
NURSE
The emperor in his rage will doom her death.
CHIRON
115 I blush to think upon this ignomy.
AARON
116 Why, there's the privilege your beauty bears.
Fie, treacherous hue, that will betray with blushing
118 The close enacts and counsels of thy heart!
119 Here's a young lad framed of another leer.
120 Look how the black slave smiles upon the father,
As who should say "Old lad, I am thine own."
122 He is your brother, lords, sensibly fed
Of that self blood that first gave life to you,
And from that womb where you imprisoned were
125 He is enfranchisèd and come to light.
126 Nay, he is your brother by the surer side,
Although my seal be stampèd in his face.
NURSE
Aaron, what shall I say unto the empress?
DEMETRIUS
Advise thee, Aaron, what is to be done,
130 And we will all subscribe to thy advice:
Save thou the child, so we may all be safe.
AARON
Then sit we down and let us all consult.
133 My son and I will have the wind of you:

---

111 *smoke* suffer   115 *ignomy* ignominy, shame   116 *privilege your beauty bears* i.e., "your white skin allows you to blush"   118 *close enacts* secret resolutions   119 *leer* complexion   122 *sensibly* perceptibly to the senses   125 *enfranchisèd* freed   126 *the surer side* i.e., the mother's side (because only mothers can be certain of their progeny)   130 *subscribe* agree   133 *have the wind of* keep watch upon (as hunters watch game, from downwind)

Keep there *[They sit.];* now talk at pleasure of your safety.

DEMETRIUS

How many women saw this child of his?

AARON

Why, so, brave lords! when we join in league,

I am a lamb, but if you brave the Moor,   137

The chaf èd boar, the mountain lioness,   138

The ocean swells not so as Aaron storms.

But say again, how many saw the child?   *140*

NURSE

Cornelia the midwife and myself,

And no one else but the delivered empress.

AARON

The empress, the midwife, and yourself:

Two may keep counsel when the third's away.

Go to the empress, tell her this I said.

   He kills her.

Weeke, weeke!

So cries a pig preparèd to the spit.

DEMETRIUS

What mean'st thou, Aaron? wherefore didst thou this?

AARON

O Lord, sir, 'tis a deed of policy!   149

Shall she live to betray this guilt of ours,   *150*

A long-tongued babbling gossip? no, lords, no.

And now be it known to you my full intent.

Not far one Muliteus my countryman   153

His wife but yesternight was brought to bed;

His child is like to her, fair as you are:

Go pack with him, and give the mother gold,   156

---

137 *brave* challenge 138 *chaf èd* enraged 149 *policy* strategy, prudence
153–54 *my countryman/His wife* i.e., my countryman's wife (The possessive
phrase is a common one, but there may be compositorial error: the lines
should perhaps read "Not far one Muly lives, my countryman,/His wife but
yesterday was brought to bed." Peele's *Battle of Alcazar*, 1589, includes a
Moor named Muley Mahomet.) 156 *pack* arrange

And tell them both the circumstance of all,
And how by this their child shall be advanced,
And be receivèd for the emperor's heir

160 And substituted in the place of mine,
To calm this tempest whirling in the court,
And let the emperor dandle him for his own.

163 Hark ye, lords: you see I have given her physic,
And you must needs bestow her funeral.

165 The fields are near, and you are gallant grooms.

166 This done, see that you take no longer days,
But send the midwife presently to me.
The midwife and the nurse well made away,
Then let the ladies tattle what they please.

CHIRON

170 Aaron, I see thou wilt not trust the air
With secrets.

DEMETRIUS   For this care of Tamora,
Herself and hers are highly bound to thee.

Exeunt [Demetrius and Chiron,
bearing off the dead Nurse].

AARON

Now to the Goths, as swift as swallow flies,
There to dispose this treasure in mine arms
And secretly to greet the empress' friends.
Come on, you thick-lipped slave, I'll bear you hence,

177 For it is you that puts us to our shifts.
I'll make you feed on berries and on roots,

179 And fat on curds and whey, and suck the goat,

180 And cabin in a cave, and bring you up
To be a warrior and command a camp.   *Exit.*

*

---

163 *given her physic* given the nurse medicine (ironic)   165 *grooms* attendants   166 *days* time   177 *puts . . . shifts* makes us resort to schemes   179
curds and whey coagulated milk (staple of a healthy country diet, according
to the Roman historian Tacitus)   180 *cabin* dwell

❧ **IV.3** *Enter Titus, Old Marcus, Young Lucius, and*
other Gentlemen, with bows, and Titus bears the ar-
rows with letters on the ends of them.

TITUS
    Come, Marcus, come; kinsmen, this is the way.
    Sir boy, let me see your archery:
    Look ye draw home enough, and 'tis there straight.   3
    Terras Astraea reliquit.   4
    Be you remembered, Marcus. She's gone, she's fled.   5
    Sirs, take you to your tools. You, cousins, shall
    Go sound the ocean, and cast your nets;
    Happily you may catch her in the sea,   8
    Yet there's as little justice as at land.
    No, Publius and Sempronius, you must do it.   10
    'Tis you must dig with mattock and with spade   11
    And pierce the inmost center of the earth;
    Then, when you come to Pluto's region,   13
    I pray you deliver him this petition.
    Tell him it is for justice and for aid,
    And that it comes from old Andronicus,
    Shaken with sorrows in ungrateful Rome.
    Ah, Rome! Well, well, I made thee miserable
    What time I threw the people's suffrages   19
    On him that thus doth tyrannize o'er me.   20
    Go, get you gone, and pray be careful all,
    And leave you not a man-of-war unsearched:
    This wicked emperor may have shipped her hence,
    And, kinsmen, then we may go pipe for justice.   24

IV.3 A public place in Rome   **3** *home enough* all the way; *straight* straightaway, immediately   **4** *Terras Astraea reliquit* Astraea, goddess of justice, has
left the earth (Ovid, *Metamorphoses,* I, 150)   **5** *Be you remembered* remember
8 *Happily* haply, perhaps   **11** *mattock* picklike tool   **13** *Pluto's region* Hades
19–20 *What time I threw . . . o'er me* when I urged support of Saturninus
24 *pipe* whistle (i.e., seek vainly)

MARCUS
    O Publius, is not this a heavy case,
    To see thy noble uncle thus distract?
PUBLIUS
    Therefore, my lords, it highly us concerns
    By day and night t' attend him carefully,
29 And feed his humor kindly as we may,
30 Till time beget some careful remedy.
MARCUS
    Kinsmen, his sorrows are past remedy.
32 [But . . .]
    Join with the Goths, and with revengeful war
34 Take wreak on Rome for this ingratitude,
    And vengeance on the traitor Saturnine.
TITUS
    Publius, how now? how now, my masters?
    What, have you met with her?
PUBLIUS
    No, my good lord; but Pluto sends you word,
    If you will have Revenge from hell, you shall.
40 Marry, for Justice, she is so employed,
    He thinks, with Jove in heaven, or somewhere else,
42 So that perforce you must needs stay a time.
TITUS
    He doth me wrong to feed me with delays.
    I'll dive into the burning lake below,
45 And pull her out of Acheron by the heels.
    Marcus, we are but shrubs, no cedars we,
47 No big-boned men framed of the Cyclops' size;
    But metal, Marcus, steel to the very back,
49 Yet wrung with wrongs more than our backs can bear;
50 And, sith there's no justice in earth nor hell,

---

29 *humor* mood   32 *[But . . .]* (A line seems to be missing from the first quarto at this point.)   34 *wreak* vengeance   42 *stay* wait   45 *Acheron* (river in Hades)   47 *Cyclops* (giants in Homer's *Odyssey*, IX)   49 *wrung* squeezed, burdened   50 *sith* since

We will solicit heaven, and move the gods
To send down Justice for to wreak our wrongs.   52
Come, to this gear. You are a good archer, Marcus.   53
  He gives them the arrows.
Ad Jovem, that's for you: here, *ad Apollinem.*   54
Ad Martem, that's for myself.
Here, boy, "to Pallas": here, "to Mercury."   56
"To Saturn," Caius, not to Saturnine;
You were as good to shoot against the wind.   58
To it, boy! Marcus, loose when I bid.   59
Of my word, I have written to effect;   60
There's not a god left unsolicited.

MARCUS
  Kinsmen, shoot all your shafts into the court:
  We will afflict the emperor in his pride.

TITUS
  Now, masters, draw. *[They shoot.]* O, well said, Lucius! 64
  Good boy, in Virgo's lap; give it Pallas.   65

MARCUS
  My lord, I aim a mile beyond the moon.
  Your letter is with Jupiter by this.   67

TITUS   Ha, ha!
  Publius, Publius, what hast thou done?
  See, see, thou hast shot off one of Taurus' horns!   70

MARCUS
  This was the sport, my lord: when Publius shot,
  The Bull, being galled, gave Aries such a knock   72
  That down fell both the Ram's horns in the court;
  And who should find them but the empress' villain?   74
  She laughed, and told the Moor he should not choose

---

52 *wreak* avenge   53 *gear* business   54–55 *Ad Jovem . . . ad Apollinem. / Ad
Martem* To Jove . . . to Apollo. To Mars   56 *Pallas* Athena (Minerva in the
Roman pantheon)   58 *You were as good* you'd do as well   59 *loose* let fly   60
Of my word on my word   64 *well said* well done   65 *Virgo* (the Virgin in the
zodiac; *Taurus,* l. 70, is the Bull, *Aries,* l. 72, the Ram; the zodiac may have
been painted on the ceiling over the stage)   67 *by this* by this time   72
galled angry, sore   74 *villain* servant (with modern sense)

76 But give them to his master for a present.

TITUS

77 Why, there it goes! God give his lordship joy!
    Enter the Clown, with a basket, and two pigeons in it.
    News, news from heaven! Marcus, the post is come.
    Sirrah, what tidings? Have you any letters?

80 Shall I have justice? what says Jupiter?

81 CLOWN Who? the gibbet-maker? He says that he hath
    taken them down again, for the man must not be
    hanged till the next week.

TITUS But what says Jupiter I ask thee?

CLOWN Alas, sir, I know not Jubiter. I never drank with
    him in all my life.

87 TITUS Why, villain, art not thou the carrier?

CLOWN Ay, of my pigeons, sir, nothing else.

TITUS Why, didst thou not come from heaven?

90 CLOWN From heaven? alas, sir, I never came there. God
    forbid I should be so bold to press to heaven in my
    young days. Why, I am going with my pigeons to the

93 tribunal plebs, to take up a matter of brawl betwixt my

94 uncle and one of the emperal's men.

95 MARCUS *[To Titus]* Why, sir, that is as fit as can be to

96 serve for your oration; and let him deliver the pigeons
    to the emperor from you.

98 ***TITUS Tell me, can you deliver an oration to the em-
    peror with a grace?

100 CLOWN Nay, truly, sir, I could never say grace in all my
    life.***

TITUS

    Sirrah, come hither: make no more ado,

---

76 *give them to his master* give the horns (sign of the cuckold) to Saturninus
77 **s.d.** *Clown* yokel 81 *gibbet-maker* gallows maker (Clown hears Titus's
Jupiter as "gibbeter") 87 *carrier* messenger 93 *tribunal plebs* Clown's error
for *"tribunus plebis,"* the people's tribune; *take up* settle 94 *emperal* Clown's
error for "emperor" 95 *that* i.e., that man 96 *oration* petition 98–101
*** . . . *** (These four lines may represent an early draft, accidentally retained in the printed text, of the following passage.)

But give your pigeons to the emperor:
By me thou shalt have justice at his hands.
Hold, hold, meanwhile here's money for thy charges.   105
Give me pen and ink.
Sirrah, can you with a grace deliver a supplication?
CLOWN Ay, sir.
TITUS Then here is a supplication for you. And when
you come to him, at the first approach you must kneel,   110
then kiss his foot, then deliver up your pigeons, and
then look for your reward. I'll be at hand, sir: see you
do it bravely.   113
CLOWN I warrant you, sir, let me alone.
TITUS
Sirrah, hast thou a knife? Come, let me see it.
Here, Marcus, fold it in the oration,
For thou hast made it like an humble suppliant.   117
And when thou hast given it to the emperor,
Knock at my door and tell me what he says.
CLOWN God be with you, sir. I will.   *Exit.*   120
TITUS Come, Marcus, let us go. Publius, follow me.
                                              Exeunt.

*

❧ **IV.4** *Enter Emperor and Empress, and her two sons.*
The Emperor brings the arrows in his hand that Titus
shot at him.

SATURNINUS
Why, lords, what wrongs are these! Was ever seen
An emperor in Rome thus overborne,   2
Troubled, confronted thus, and, for the extent   3
Of egal justice, used in such contempt?

---

105 *Hold, hold* wait a minute; *charges* expenses **113** *bravely* well **117** *hast made* (a problematic phrase; a suggested emendation is "For thou *must hold* it like an humble suppliant")

IV.4 Before Saturninus's palace **2** *overborne* oppressed **3–4** *for the extent / Of egal* for the exercise of equal

My lords, you know, as know the mightful gods,
However these disturbers of our peace
Buzz in the people's ears, there naught hath passed,
8 But even with law, against the willful sons
Of old Andronicus. And what an if
10 His sorrows have so overwhelmed his wits?
11 Shall we be thus afflicted in his wreaks,
His fits, his frenzy, and his bitterness?
And now he writes to heaven for his redress.
See, here's "to Jove," and this "to Mercury,"
This "to Apollo," this "to the god of war":
Sweet scrolls to fly about the streets of Rome!
What's this but libeling against the Senate
18 And blazoning our unjustice everywhere?
A goodly humor, is it not, my lords?
20 As who would say, in Rome no justice were.
21 But if I live, his feignèd ecstasies
Shall be no shelter to these outrages;
23 But he and his shall know that justice lives
In Saturninus' health, whom, if he sleep,
He'll so awake as he in fury shall
Cut off the proud'st conspirator that lives.

TAMORA
My gracious lord, my lovely Saturnine,
Lord of my life, commander of my thoughts,
Calm thee, and bear the faults of Titus' age,
30 Th' effects of sorrow for his valiant sons,
Whose loss hath pierced him deep and scarred his
      heart;
And rather comfort his distressèd plight
33 Than prosecute the meanest or the best

---

8 *even with* according to; *willful* (1) lustful ("will" = sexual appetite), (2) headstrong **11** *wreaks* vindictive acts **18** *blazoning* proclaiming **21** *ecstasies* fits of madness **23–26** *But he . . . that lives* (The confusion of pronouns may indicate textual corruption: the sense is that if Justice sleeps, the emperor will awaken Justice and cause him to take vengeance on the conspirators.) **33** *the meanest or the best* person of lowest or highest rank

For these contempts. *[Aside]* Why, thus it shall become
High-witted Tamora to gloze with all.   35
But, Titus, I have touched thee to the quick;
Thy lifeblood out, if Aaron now be wise,   37
Then is all safe, the anchor in the port.
    Enter Clown.
How now, good fellow? Wouldst thou speak with us?
CLOWN   Yea, forsooth, an your mistress-ship be empe-   40
rial.
TAMORA
Empress I am, but yonder sits the emperor.
CLOWN   'Tis he. God and Saint Stephen give you god-   43
den. I have brought you a letter and a couple of pigeons
here.
    He [Saturninus] reads the letter.
SATURNINUS
Go take him away, and hang him presently.
CLOWN   How much money must I have?
TAMORA   Come, sirrah, you must be hanged.
CLOWN   Hanged? By' lady, then I have brought up a   49
neck to a fair end.   *Exit.*   50
SATURNINUS
Despiteful and intolerable wrongs!
Shall I endure this monstrous villainy?
I know from whence this same device proceeds.
May this be borne as if his traitorous sons,
That died by law for murder of our brother,
Have by my means been butchered wrongfully?
Go drag the villain hither by the hair;
Nor age nor honor shall shape privilege.   58
For this proud mock I'll be thy slaughterman,
Sly frantic wretch, that holp'st to make me great   60

---

35 *gloze* speak deceptively   **37** *Thy lifeblood out* once thy lifeblood is spilled
43–44 *godden* good evening (used after noon)   **49** *By' lady* (interjection,
from "by Our Lady")   **58** *shape privilege* create immunity   **60** *that holp'st to
make me great* who helped me to the throne

61   In hope thyself should govern Rome and me!
         Enter Nuntius Aemilius.
      What news with thee, Aemilius?
AEMILIUS
      Arm, my lords! Rome never had more cause.
64   The Goths have gathered head, and with a power
      Of high-resolvèd men, bent to the spoil,
66   They hither march amain, under conduct
      Of Lucius, son to old Andronicus,
      Who threats in course of this revenge to do
69   As much as ever Coriolanus did.
SATURNINUS
70   Is warlike Lucius general of the Goths?
      These tidings nip me, and I hang the head
      As flowers with frost or grass beat down with storms.
      Ay, now begins our sorrows to approach.
      'Tis he the common people love so much;
      Myself hath often overheard them say,
      When I have walkèd like a private man,
      That Lucius' banishment was wrongfully,
      And they have wished that Lucius were their emperor.
TAMORA
      Why should you fear? is not your city strong?
SATURNINUS
80   Ay, but the citizens favor Lucius
      And will revolt from me to succor him.
TAMORA
82   King, be thy thoughts imperious like thy name.
      Is the sun dimmed, that gnats do fly in it?
      The eagle suffers little birds to sing,
85   And is not careful what they mean thereby,

---

61 s.d. *Nuntius* messenger (Latin) 64 *gathered head* raised an army 66
amain at full speed; *conduct* leadership 69 *Coriolanus* exiled Roman hero
who led an army against Rome (subject of one of Shakespeare's last tragedies)
82 *thy name* i.e., Saturninus, from "Saturn" 85 *careful* concerned

Knowing that with the shadow of his wings
He can at pleasure stint their melody: 87
Even so mayest thou the giddy men of Rome.
Then cheer thy spirit, for know thou, emperor,
I will enchant the old Andronicus   90
With words more sweet, and yet more dangerous,
Than baits to fish or honey stalks to sheep,   92
When as the one is wounded with the bait,
The other rotted with delicious feed.

SATURNINUS
But he will not entreat his son for us.

TAMORA
If Tamora entreat him, then he will;
For I can smooth, and fill his agèd ears   97
With golden promises, that, were his heart
Almost impregnable, his old ears deaf,
Yet should both ear and heart obey my tongue.   100
   [To Aemilius]
Go thou before to be our ambassador;
Say that the emperor requests a parley
Of warlike Lucius, and appoint the meeting
Even at his father's house, the old Andronicus.

SATURNINUS
Aemilius, do this message honorably,
And if he stand in hostage for his safety,   106
Bid him demand what pledge will please him best.

AEMILIUS
Your bidding shall I do effectually.   *Exit.*

TAMORA
Now will I to that old Andronicus
And temper him with all the art I have,   110
To pluck proud Lucius from the warlike Goths.

---

87 *stint* stop   92 *honey stalks* clover flowers (eating too much can make sheep ill)   97 *smooth* flatter   106 *stand in* insist upon   110 *temper* work upon

And now, sweet emperor, be blithe again
And bury all thy fear in my devices.

SATURNINUS

114 Then go successantly, and plead to him.   *Exeunt.*

                                    *

∾ **V.1** *Enter Lucius, with an army of Goths, with Drums
and Soldiers.*

LUCIUS

1 Approvèd warriors and my faithful friends,
I have receivèd letters from great Rome
Which signifies what hate they bear their emperor
And how desirous of our sight they are.
Therefore, great lords, be as your titles witness,
Imperious, and impatient of your wrongs;

7 And wherein Rome hath done you any scath,
Let him make treble satisfaction.

[FIRST] GOTH

9 Brave slip sprung from the great Andronicus,
10 Whose name was once our terror, now our comfort,
Whose high exploits and honorable deeds
Ingrateful Rome requites with foul contempt,

13 Be bold in us: we'll follow where thou lead'st,
Like stinging bees in hottest summer's day,
Led by their master to the flowered fields,
And be avenged on cursèd Tamora.

[ALL]

And as he saith, so say we all with him.

LUCIUS

I humbly thank him, and I thank you all.

19 But who comes here, led by a lusty Goth?

---

114 *successantly* in succession (?) (the word is not found elsewhere and may
be an error for "incessantly" – immediately)

   V.1 Fields near Rome 1 *Approvèd* tested 7 *scath* harm 9 *slip* offshoot
13 *bold* confident 19 *lusty* strong, vigorous

> *Enter a Goth, leading of Aaron with his Child in his*
>   *arms.*

[SECOND] GOTH

Renownèd Lucius, from our troops I strayed   20
To gaze upon a ruinous monastery,
And as I earnestly did fix mine eye
Upon the wasted building, suddenly
I heard a child cry underneath a wall.
I made unto the noise, when soon I heard
The crying babe controlled with this discourse: 26
"Peace, tawny slave, half me and half thy dame.   27
Did not thy hue bewray whose brat thou art,   28
Had nature lent thee but thy mother's look,
Villain, thou mightst have been an emperor: 30
But where the bull and cow are both milk-white,
They never do beget a coal-black calf.
Peace, villain, peace!" even thus he rates the babe,   33
"For I must bear thee to a trusty Goth,
Who, when he knows thou art the empress' babe,
Will hold thee dearly for thy mother's sake."
With this, my weapon drawn, I rushed upon him,
Surprised him suddenly, and brought him hither
To use as you think needful of the man.

LUCIUS

O worthy Goth, this is the incarnate devil   40
That robbed Andronicus of his good hand:
This is the pearl that pleased your empress' eye;
And here's the base fruit of her burning lust.
Say, wall-eyed slave, whither wouldst thou convey   44
This growing image of thy fiendlike face?
Why dost not speak? What, deaf? not a word?
A halter, soldiers! Hang him on this tree,

---

26 *controlled* calmed   27 *tawny* dark; *slave* (used affectionately, as are the following insults, "brat" and "villain")   28 i.e., if your color didn't reveal your black father   33 *rates* berates, scolds   44 *wall-eyed* glaring (literally, having a discolored eye)

And by his side his fruit of bastardy.

AARON
Touch not the boy, he is of royal blood.

LUCIUS
50   Too like the sire for ever being good.
51   First hang the child, that he may see it sprawl –
A sight to vex the father's soul withal.
Get me a ladder.
[A ladder brought, which Aaron is made to climb]

AARON   Lucius, save the child,
And bear it from me to the empress.
If thou do this, I'll show thee wondrous things
That highly may advantage thee to hear;
If thou wilt not, befall what may befall,
I'll speak no more – but vengeance rot you all!

LUCIUS
Say on, and if it please me which thou speak'st,
60   Thy child shall live, and I will see it nourished.

AARON
And if it please thee! why, assure thee, Lucius,
'Twill vex thy soul to hear what I shall speak;
For I must talk of murders, rapes, and massacres,
Acts of black night, abominable deeds,
Complots of mischief, treason, villainies
66   Ruthful to hear, yet piteously performed;
And this shall all be buried in my death
Unless thou swear to me my child shall live.

LUCIUS
Tell on thy mind; I say thy child shall live.

AARON
70   Swear that he shall, and then I will begin.

LUCIUS
Who should I swear by? thou believest no god.
That granted, how canst thou believe an oath?

---

50 *for ever being* ever to be   **51** *sprawl* convulse (in death)   **66** *Ruthful*
lamentable; *piteously* so as to arouse pity

AARON
    What if I do not? as indeed I do not.
    Yet, for I know thou art religious
    And hast a thing within thee callèd conscience,
    With twenty popish tricks and ceremonies   76
    Which I have seen thee careful to observe,
    Therefore I urge thy oath. For that I know
    An idiot holds his bauble for a god   79
    And keeps the oath which by that god he swears,   80
    To that I'll urge him: therefore thou shalt vow
    By that same god, what god soe'er it be,
    That thou adorest and hast in reverence,
    To save my boy, to nourish and bring him up,   84
    Or else I will discover naught to thee.
LUCIUS
    Even by my god I swear to thee I will.
AARON
    First know thou, I begot him on the empress.
LUCIUS
    O most insatiate and luxurious woman!   88
AARON
    Tut, Lucius, this was but a deed of charity
    To that which thou shalt hear of me anon.   90
    'Twas her two sons that murdered Bassianus;
    They cut thy sister's tongue, and ravished her,
    And cut her hands, and trimmed her as thou sawest. 93
LUCIUS
    O detestable villain! call'st thou that trimming?
AARON
    Why, she was washed and cut and trimmed, and 'twas
    Trim sport for them which had the doing of it.   96

---

76 *popish tricks* (Aaron's dig at Catholic ritual: such anachronisms are common in Shakespeare) 79 *holds his bauble for a god* worships his jester's stick
84 *nourish* (monosyllabic) variant form of "nurse" 88 *luxurious* lustful 90
To compared to; *anon* in a moment 93 *trimmed* dressed, "fixed her up" (in
addition to "cut") 96 *Trim* fine

LUCIUS
    O barbarous beastly villains like thyself!

AARON
    Indeed, I was their tutor to instruct them.
99   That codding spirit had they from their mother,
100   As sure a card as ever won the set;
    That bloody mind I think they learned of me,
102   As true a dog as ever fought at head.
    Well, let my deeds be witness of my worth.
104   I trained thy brethren to that guileful hole
    Where the dead corpse of Bassianus lay.
    I wrote the letter that thy father found
    And hid the gold within that letter mentioned,
    Confederate with the queen and her two sons;
    And what not done, that thou hast cause to rue,
110   Wherein I had no stroke of mischief in it?
111   I played the cheater for thy father's hand,
    And when I had it, drew myself apart
    And almost broke my heart with extreme laughter.
114   I pried me through the crevice of a wall
    When for his hand he had his two sons' heads,
    Beheld his tears, and laughed so heartily
    That both mine eyes were rainy like to his;
    And when I told the empress of this sport,
119   She sounded almost at my pleasing tale
120   And for my tidings gave me twenty kisses.

GOTH
    What, canst thou say all this and never blush?

AARON
122   Ay, like a black dog, as the saying is.

LUCIUS
    Art thou not sorry for these heinous deeds?

---

99 *codding* lustful, sexy (from "cod," slang for testicle)   100 *set* game   102 *at head* (a reference to bull-baiting, in which a brave dog bit the bull at the nose)   104 *trained* lured   111 *cheater* swindler, but also "escheator," officer who supervised property forfeited to the crown   114 *pried me* spied   119 *sounded* swooned, fainted   122 *like a black dog* i.e., not at all

AARON
    Ay, that I had not done a thousand more.
    Even now I curse the day, and yet I think   125
    Few come within the compass of my curse,
    Wherein I did not some notorious ill:
    As kill a man, or else devise his death;
    Ravish a maid, or plot the way to do it;
    Accuse some innocent, and forswear myself;   130
    Set deadly enmity between two friends;
    Make poor men's cattle break their necks;
    Set fire on barns and haystacks in the night
    And bid the owners quench them with their tears.
    Oft have I digged up dead men from their graves
    And set them upright at their dear friends' door
    Even when their sorrows almost was forgot,   137
    And on their skins, as on the bark of trees,
    Have with my knife carvèd in Roman letters
    "Let not your sorrow die, though I am dead."   *140*
    But I have done a thousand dreadful things
    As willingly as one would kill a fly,
    And nothing grieves me heartily indeed
    But that I cannot do ten thousand more.
LUCIUS
    Bring down the devil, for he must not die
    So sweet a death as hanging presently.
    [Aaron is brought down from the ladder.]
AARON
    If there be devils, would I were a devil,
    To live and burn in everlasting fire,
    So I might have your company in hell
    But to torment you with my bitter tongue!   *150*
LUCIUS
    Sirs, stop his mouth and let him speak no more.

125–26 *and yet . . . curse* i.e., my curse on days when I did no evil includes
very few days   130 *forswear* perjure   137 *their sorrows* grief over the friends'
death

Enter Aemilius.

GOTH
  My lord, there is a messenger from Rome
  Desires to be admitted to your presence.

LUCIUS
  Let him come near.
  Welcome, Aemilius: what's the news from Rome?

AEMILIUS
  Lord Lucius, and you princes of the Goths,
  The Roman emperor greets you all by me,
  And, for he understands you are in arms,
  He craves a parley at your father's house,
160 Willing you to demand your hostages,
  And they shall be immediately delivered.

GOTH
  What says our general?

LUCIUS
  Aemilius, let the emperor give his pledges
  Unto my father and my uncle Marcus,
  And we will come. March, away.   *[Exeunt.]*

*

  ❧ **V.2** *Enter Tamora and her two sons, disguised.*

TAMORA
1 Thus, in this strange and sad habiliment,
  I will encounter with Andronicus,
  And say I am Revenge, sent from below
  To join with him and right his heinous wrongs.
5 Knock at his study, where they say he keeps
  To ruminate strange plots of dire revenge.
  Tell him Revenge is come to join with him
  And work confusion on his enemies.
    They knock, and Titus opens his study door.

V.2 Before the house of Titus   **1** *sad habiliment* somber clothing   **5** *keeps* stays

TITUS
    Who doth molest my contemplation?
    Is it your trick to make me ope the door,   *10*
    That so my sad decrees may fly away   11
    And all my study be to no effect?   12
    You are deceived; for what I mean to do
    See here in bloody lines I have set down;
    And what is written shall be executed.
TAMORA
    Titus, I am come to talk with thee.
TITUS
    No, not a word. How can I grace my talk,
    Wanting a hand to give it action?   18
    Thou hast the odds of me, therefore no more.   19
TAMORA
    If thou didst know me, thou wouldst talk with me. *20*
TITUS
    I am not mad; I know thee well enough.
    Witness this wretched stump, witness these crimson
      lines,
    Witness these trenches made by grief and care,   23
    Witness the tiring day and heavy night,
    Witness all sorrow, that I know thee well
    For our proud empress, mighty Tamora.
    Is not thy coming for my other hand?
TAMORA
    Know, thou sad man, I am not Tamora;
    She is thy enemy, and I thy friend.
    I am Revenge, sent from th' infernal kingdom   *30*
    To ease the gnawing vulture of thy mind   31
    By working wreakful vengeance on thy foes.   32
    Come down and welcome me to this world's light;

---

11 *sad decrees* serious resolutions   12 *study* planning   18 lacking a hand to gesture ("give it action" is F's alteration of Q's "give that accord")   19 *odds of* advantage over   23 *trenches* wrinkles   31 *gnawing vulture* (alluding to the vulture that daily fed on the liver of the bound Prometheus)   32 *wreakful* punishing, painful

Confer with me of murder and of death.
There's not a hollow cave or lurking place,
No vast obscurity or misty vale,
Where bloody murder or detested rape
38 Can couch for fear, but I will find them out,
And in their ears tell them my dreadful name,
40 Revenge, which makes the foul offender quake.

TITUS
Art thou Revenge? and art thou sent to me
To be a torment to mine enemies?

TAMORA
I am; therefore come down and welcome me.

TITUS
Do me some service ere I come to thee.
Lo, by thy side where Rape and Murder stands;
Now give some surance that thou art Revenge:
Stab them, or tear them on thy chariot wheels,
And then I'll come and be thy wagoner
And whirl along with thee about the globe.
50 Provide thee two proper palfreys, black as jet,
To hale thy vengeful wagon swift away
And find out murderers in their guilty caves;
53 And when thy car is loaden with their heads,
I will dismount, and by thy wagon wheel
Trot like a servile footman all day long,
56 Even from Hyperion's rising in the east
Until his very downfall in the sea;
And day by day I'll do this heavy task,
59 So thou destroy Rapine and Murder there.

TAMORA
60 These are my ministers and come with me.

TITUS
Are they thy ministers? what are they called?

---

38 *couch* lie hidden   50 *proper palfreys* handsome horses   53 *car* chariot
56 *Hyperion* the sun god   59 *So* provided that; *Rapine* raped

TAMORA
   Rape and Murder; therefore callèd so
   'Cause they take vengeance of such kind of men.
TITUS
   Good Lord, how like the empress' sons they are!
   And you the empress! but we worldly men   65
   Have miserable, mad, mistaking eyes.
   O sweet Revenge, now do I come to thee,
   And, if one arm's embracement will content thee,
   I will embrace thee in it by and by.   [Exit.]
TAMORA
   This closing with him fits his lunacy.   70
   Whate'er I forge to feed his brainsick humors   71
   Do you uphold and maintain in your speeches,
   For now he firmly takes me for Revenge;
   And, being credulous in this mad thought,
   I'll make him send for Lucius his son,
   And whilst I at a banquet hold him sure,   76
   I'll find some cunning practice out of hand   77
   To scatter and disperse the giddy Goths,
   Or at the least make them his enemies.
   See, here he comes, and I must ply my theme.   80
     [Enter Titus.]
TITUS
   Long have I been forlorn, and all for thee.
   Welcome, dread Fury, to my woeful house.
   Rapine and Murder, you are welcome too.
   How like the empress and her sons you are!
   Well are you fitted, had you but a Moor.
   Could not all hell afford you such a devil?
   For well I wot the empress never wags   87
   But in her company there is a Moor,
   And, would you represent our queen aright,

---

65 *worldly* mortal   70 *closing* agreeing   71 *forge* invent   76 *hold him sure*
keep him safe   77 *practice* scheme; *out of hand* on the spur of the moment
80 *ply my theme* tend to my business   87 *wags* moves

90   It were convenient you had such a devil.
        But welcome as you are: what shall we do?

TAMORA
        What wouldst thou have us do, Andronicus?

DEMETRIUS
        Show me a murderer, I'll deal with him.

CHIRON
        Show me a villain that hath done a rape,
        And I am sent to be revenged on him.

TAMORA
        Show me a thousand that hath done thee wrong,
        And I will be revengèd on them all.

TITUS   *[To Demetrius]*
        Look round about the wicked streets of Rome,
        And when thou find'st a man that's like thyself,
100   Good Murder, stab him; he's a murderer.
            [To Chiron]
101   Go thou with him, and when it is thy hap
        To find another that is like to thee,
        Good Rapine, stab him; he is a ravisher.
            [To Tamora]
        Go thou with them, and in the emperor's court
        There is a queen, attended by a Moor.
        Well shalt thou know her by thine own proportion,
        For up and down she doth resemble thee.
        I pray thee do on them some violent death;
        They have been violent to me and mine.

TAMORA
110   Well hast thou lessoned us; this shall we do.
        But would it please thee, good Andronicus,
        To send for Lucius, thy thrice-valiant son,
        Who leads towards Rome a band of warlike Goths,
        And bid him come and banquet at thy house:
        When he is here, even at thy solemn feast,
        I will bring in the empress and her sons,

----

90 *convenient* fitting   101 *hap* chance

The emperor himself, and all thy foes,
And at thy mercy shall they stoop and kneel,
And on them shalt thou ease thy angry heart.
What says Andronicus to this device?   120

TITUS
Marcus, my brother, 'tis sad Titus calls.
    Enter Marcus.
Go, gentle Marcus, to thy nephew Lucius;
Thou shalt enquire him out among the Goths.
Bid him repair to me and bring with him   124
Some of the chiefest princes of the Goths.
Bid him encamp his soldiers where they are.
Tell him the emperor and the empress too
Feast at my house, and he shall feast with them.
This do thou for my love, and so let him,
As he regards his agèd father's life.   130

MARCUS
This will I do and soon return again.   *[Exit.]*

TAMORA
Now will I hence about thy business
And take my ministers along with me.

TITUS
Nay, nay, let Rape and Murder stay with me,
Or else I'll call my brother back again
And cleave to no revenge but Lucius.   136

TAMORA   *[Aside to her sons]*
What say you, boys? will you abide with him
Whiles I go tell my lord the emperor
How I have governed our determined jest?   139
Yield to his humor, smooth and speak him fair,   140
And tarry with him till I turn again.

TITUS   *[Aside]*
I knew them all, though they supposed me mad,

---

124 *repair* come, return   136 *cleave* cling   139 *governed . . . jest* arranged
the trick we agreed on   140 *smooth . . . fair* flatter and humor him

143   And will o'erreach them in their own devices,
       A pair of cursèd hellhounds and their dame.
DEMETRIUS
       Madam, depart at pleasure; leave us here.
TAMORA
       Farewell, Andronicus. Revenge now goes
147   To lay a complot to betray thy foes.
TITUS
       I know thou dost; and, sweet Revenge, farewell.
                                        [Exit Tamora.]

CHIRON
       Tell us, old man, how shall we be employed?
TITUS
150   Tut, I have work enough for you to do.
       Publius, come hither, Caius and Valentine.
         [Enter Publius, Caius, and Valentine.]
PUBLIUS
       What is your will?
TITUS
       Know you these two?
PUBLIUS
       The empress' sons, I take them, Chiron and Demetrius.
TITUS
       Fie, Publius, fie! thou art too much deceived.
       The one is Murder, and Rape is the other's name,
       And therefore bind them, gentle Publius:
       Caius and Valentine, lay hands on them.
       Oft have you heard me wish for such an hour,
160   And now I find it. Therefore bind them sure,
       And stop their mouths if they begin to cry.   *[Exit.]*
CHIRON
       Villains, forbear! we are the empress' sons.
PUBLIUS
       And therefore do we what we are commanded.
       Stop close their mouths, let them not speak a word.

_____

143 *o'erreach* outwit   **147** *complot* plot

Is he sure bound? look that you bind them fast.
Enter Titus Andronicus with a knife, and Lavinia
with a basin.

TITUS

Come, come, Lavinia; look, thy foes are bound.
Sirs, stop their mouths, let them not speak to me,
But let them hear what fearful words I utter.
O villains, Chiron and Demetrius!
Here stands the spring whom you have stained with   *170*
   mud,
This goodly summer with your winter mixed.
You killed her husband, and for that vile fault
Two of her brothers were condemned to death,
My hand cut off and made a merry jest;
Both her sweet hands, her tongue, and that more dear
Than hands or tongue, her spotless chastity,
Inhuman traitors, you constrained and forced.   177
What would you say if I should let you speak?
Villains, for shame you could not beg for grace.
Hark, wretches, how I mean to martyr you.   180
This one hand yet is left to cut your throats
Whiles that Lavinia 'tween her stumps doth hold
The basin that receives your guilty blood.
You know your mother means to feast with me,
And calls herself Revenge, and thinks me mad.
Hark, villains, I will grind your bones to dust,
And with your blood and it I'll make a paste,
And of the paste a coffin I will rear,   188
And make two pasties of your shameful heads,   189
And bid that strumpet, your unhallowed dam,   *190*
Like to the earth, swallow her own increase.   191
This is the feast that I have bid her to,
And this the banquet she shall surfeit on,
For worse than Philomel you used my daughter,

---

177 *constrained* violated   180 *martyr* kill violently   188 *coffin* pie-crust
189 *pasties* meat pies   191 *increase* offspring

195 And worse than Procne I will be revenged.
And now prepare your throats. Lavinia, come,
Receive the blood; and when that they are dead,
Let me go grind their bones to powder small
199 And with this hateful liquor temper it,
200 And in that paste let their vile heads be baked.
201 Come, come, be everyone officious
To make this banquet, which I wish may prove
203 More stern and bloody than the Centaurs' feast.
        He cuts their throats.
So, now bring them in, for I'll play the cook
205 And see them ready against their mother comes.
                                                Exeunt.

                                  *

∾ V.3 *Enter Lucius, Marcus, and the Goths [with Aaron
     prisoner, and his Child in the arms of an Attendant].*

LUCIUS
    Uncle Marcus, since 'tis my father's mind
    That I repair to Rome, I am content.
GOTH
    And ours with thine, befall what fortune will.
LUCIUS
    Good uncle, take you in this barbarous Moor,
    This ravenous tiger, this accursèd devil.
6   Let him receive no sustenance, fetter him,
    Till he be brought unto the empress' face
    For testimony of her foul proceedings.

---

195 *Procne* (wife of Tereus, who raped and mutilated her sister Philomel: to
avenge that act, Procne killed her son Itys and fed him to his father) 199
temper blend 201 *officious* efficient, busy 203 *Centaurs' feast* (the Centaurs, invited by the Lapiths to the wedding celebration of Pirithous and
Hippodamia, were slaughtered by their hosts) 205 *against* by the time that
V.3 Titus's house 6 *fetter* bind

And see the ambush of our friends be strong;   9
I fear the emperor means no good to us.   10

AARON

Some devil whisper curses in mine ear
And prompt me that my tongue may utter forth
The venomous malice of my swelling heart!   13

LUCIUS

Away, inhuman dog, unhallowed slave!   14
Sirs, help our uncle to convey him in.
                              [Exeunt Goths with Aaron.]
The trumpets show the emperor is at hand.
    *Sound trumpets. Enter Emperor and Empress, with
    [Aemilius,] Tribunes, and others.*

SATURNINUS

What, hath the firmament more suns than one?   17

LUCIUS

What boots it thee to call thyself a sun?   18

MARCUS

Rome's emperor, and nephew, break the parle;   19
These quarrels must be quietly debated.   20
The feast is ready which the careful Titus   21
Hath ordained to an honorable end,
For peace, for love, for league, and good to Rome.
Please you therefore draw nigh and take your places.

SATURNINUS

Marcus, we will.
    *[A table brought in.] Trumpets sounding, enter Titus
    like a cook, placing the dishes, and Lavinia with a veil
    over her face.*

TITUS

Welcome, my lord; welcome, dread queen;

---

9 *ambush* the troops preparing for the attack   13 *swelling* overcharged (*malice*, or envy, was thought to expand and tax the heart)   14 *unhallowed* im-
pure (here, foreign, un-Roman)   17 *firmament* sky   18 *boots* avails   19
break the parle break off the dispute   21 *careful* full of sorrows (perhaps also
with modern sense)

Welcome, ye warlike Goths; welcome, Lucius;
28 And welcome all: although the cheer be poor,
    'Twill fill your stomachs; please you eat of it.

SATURNINUS
30 Why art thou thus attired, Andronicus?

TITUS
    Because I would be sure to have all well
    To entertain your highness and your empress.

TAMORA
    We are beholding to you, good Andronicus.

TITUS
34 And if your highness knew my heart, you were.
35 My lord the emperor, resolve me this:
36 Was it well done of rash Virginius
    To slay his daughter with his own right hand,
38 Because she was enforced, stained, and deflowered?

SATURNINUS
    It was, Andronicus.

TITUS
40 Your reason, mighty lord?

SATURNINUS
41 Because the girl should not survive her shame,
    And by her presence still renew his sorrows.

TITUS
    A reason mighty, strong, and effectual;
44 A pattern, precedent, and lively warrant
    For me, most wretched, to perform the like.
    Die, die, Lavinia, and thy shame with thee,
    And with thy shame thy father's sorrow die!
    [He kills her.]

SATURNINUS
48 What hast thou done, unnatural and unkind?

---

28 *cheer* offerings, food   **34** *And if* if   **35** *resolve* answer   **36** *Virginius* (Roman who killed his daughter to save her from the shame of rape; in another version he kills her to prevent the rape itself)   **38** *enforced* raped   **41** *Because* so that   **44** *lively* vivid   **48** *unkind* cruel, inhuman

TITUS
   Killed her for whom my tears have made me blind.
   I am as woeful as Virginius was,   50
   And have a thousand times more cause than he
   To do this outrage; and it now is done.
SATURNINUS
   What, was she ravished? tell who did the deed.
TITUS
   Will't please you eat? will't please your highness feed?
TAMORA
   Why hast thou slain thine only daughter thus?
TITUS
   Not I: 'twas Chiron and Demetrius,
   They ravished her and cut away her tongue,
   And they, 'twas they, that did her all this wrong.
SATURNINUS
   Go fetch them hither to us presently.   59
TITUS
   Why, there they are, both bakèd in this pie,   60
   Whereof their mother daintily hath fed,
   Eating the flesh that she herself hath bred.
   'Tis true, 'tis true; witness my knife's sharp point!
     He stabs the Empress.
SATURNINUS
   Die, frantic wretch, for this accursèd deed!   64
     [He stabs Titus.]
LUCIUS
   Can the son's eye behold his father bleed?
   There's meed for meed, death for a deadly deed!   66
     [He stabs Saturninus.]
MARCUS
   You sad-faced men, people and sons of Rome,
   By uproar severed, as a flight of fowl
   Scattered by winds and high tempestuous gusts,

---

59 *presently* immediately   **64** *frantic* insane   **66** *meed for meed* measure for
measure (i.e., fitting reward)

70 O, let me teach you how to knit again
    This scattered corn into one mutual sheaf,
    These broken limbs again into one body.

ROMAN LORD

73 Let Rome herself be bane unto herself,
    And she whom mighty kingdoms curtsy to,
    Like a forlorn and desperate castaway,
    Do shameful execution on herself,
77 But if my frosty signs and chaps of age,
    Grave witnesses of true experience,
    Cannot induce you to attend my words,
        [To Lucius]
80 Speak, Rome's dear friend, as erst our ancestor,
    When with his solemn tongue he did discourse
82 To lovesick Dido's sad-attending ear
83 The story of that baleful burning night
    When subtle Greeks surprised King Priam's Troy.
85 Tell us what Sinon hath bewitched our ears,
    Or who hath brought the fatal engine in
87 That gives our Troy, our Rome, the civil wound.
88 My heart is not compact of flint nor steel;
    Nor can I utter all our bitter grief,
90 But floods of tears will drown my oratory
    And break my utterance, even in the time
    When it should move ye to attend me most,
    And force you to commiseration.
    Here's Rome's young captain, let him tell the tale,
    While I stand by and weep to hear him speak.

LUCIUS

96 Then, gracious auditory, be it known to you
    That Chiron and the damned Demetrius

---

70 *knit* bind together   73 *bane* poison   77 *But if* unless; *frosty signs* white
hair; *chaps* wrinkles   80 *erst* formerly; *our ancestor* i.e., Aeneas, who told the
sad tale of Troy to *Dido* (l. 82), Queen of Carthage   82 *sad-attending* seri-
ously listening   83 *baleful* evil   85 *Sinon* cunning Greek who persuaded the
Trojans to admit the wooden horse   87 *civil* incurred in civil war   88 *compact* composed   96 *auditory* audience

Were they that murderèd our emperor's brother,
And they it were that ravishèd our sister.
For their fell faults our brothers were beheaded,   100
Our father's tears despised, and basely cozened   101
Of that true hand that fought Rome's quarrel out
And sent her enemies unto the grave.
Lastly, myself unkindly banishèd,   104
The gates shut on me, and turned weeping out
To beg relief among Rome's enemies,
Who drowned their enmity in my true tears   107
And oped their arms to embrace me as a friend:
I am the turnèd-forth, be it known to you,   109
That have preserved her welfare in my blood   *110*
And from her bosom took the enemy's point,
Sheathing the steel in my adventurous body.
Alas, you know I am no vaunter, I;   113
My scars can witness, dumb although they are,   114
That my report is just and full of truth.
But soft, methinks I do digress too much,   116
Citing my worthless praise. O, pardon me!
For when no friends are by, men praise themselves.

MARCUS
Now is my turn to speak. Behold the child:
Of this was Tamora deliverèd,   *120*
The issue of an irreligious Moor,   121
Chief architect and plotter of these woes.
The villain is alive in Titus' house,
And as he is to witness, this is true.   124
Now judge what cause had Titus to revenge
These wrongs unspeakable, past patience,
Or more than any living man could bear.
Now you have heard the truth, what say you, Romans?

---

100 *fell* savage   101 *cozened* cheated   104 *unkindly* unnaturally   107 *en-mity* hatred   109 *turnèd-forth* exile   113 *vaunter* braggart   114 *dumb* mute   116 *soft* stay, wait (common imperative for silence; "hold on")   121 *irreli-gious* wicked, here un-Roman (see *unhallowed*, l. 14)   124 *to witness* to con-firm

129 Have we done aught amiss, show us wherein,
130 And, from the place where you behold us pleading,
     The poor remainder of Andronici
132 Will hand in hand all headlong hurl ourselves
133 And on the ragged stones beat forth our souls,
134 And make a mutual closure of our house.
     Speak, Romans, speak, and if you say we shall,
     Lo, hand in hand, Lucius and I will fall.

AEMILIUS
     Come, come, thou reverend man of Rome,
     And bring our emperor gently in thy hand –
     Lucius our emperor, for well I know
140 The common voice do cry it shall be so.

ALL
     Lucius, all hail, Rome's royal emperor!

MARCUS
     Go, go into old Titus' sorrowful house,
143 And hither hale that misbelieving Moor
     To be adjudged some direful slaughtering death,
     As punishment for his most wicked life.
                                        [Exeunt Attendants.]

ALL
     Lucius, all hail, Rome's gracious governor!

LUCIUS
     Thanks, gentle Romans: may I govern so
     To heal Rome's harms and wipe away her woe.
149 But, gentle people, give me aim awhile,
150 For nature puts me to a heavy task.
     Stand all aloof; but, uncle, draw you near
152 To shed obsequious tears upon this trunk.
     O, take this warm kiss on thy pale cold lips,
     These sorrowful drops upon thy bloodstained face,

---

129 *Have we done* if we have done   132 *headlong hurl ourselves* (Rome pun-
ished its traitors by throwing them from the Tarpeian rock on the Capitoline
Hill)   133 *ragged* rough   134 *mutual closure of our house* common end of
the familial line   143 *hale* drag   149 *give me aim* bear with me   152 *obsequious* funereal (from "obsequies," funeral rites)

The last true duties of thy noble son!

MARCUS

Tear for tear, and loving kiss for kiss,
Thy brother Marcus tenders on thy lips.
O, were the sum of these that I should pay
Countless and infinite, yet would I pay them.

LUCIUS

Come hither, boy; come, come and learn of us   *160*
To melt in showers: thy grandsire loved thee well.
Many a time he danced thee on his knee,
Sung thee asleep, his loving breast thy pillow.
Many a story hath he told to thee,
And bid thee bear his pretty tales in mind
And talk of them when he was dead and gone.

MARCUS

How many thousand times hath these poor lips,
When they were living, warmed themselves on thine!
O, now, sweet boy, give them their latest kiss.   169
Bid him farewell; commit him to the grave;   *170*
Do them that kindness, and take leave of them.   171

BOY

O grandsire, grandsire! ev'n with all my heart
Would I were dead, so you did live again!
O Lord, I cannot speak to him for weeping;
My tears will choke me if I ope my mouth.
    [Enter Attendants with Aaron.]

ROMAN

You sad Andronici, have done with woes.
Give sentence on this execrable wretch
That hath been breeder of these dire events.

LUCIUS

Set him breast-deep in earth, and famish him.   179
There let him stand and rave and cry for food.   *180*
If any one relieves or pities him,

---

169 *latest* last   **171** *them* i.e., Titus's lips   **179** *famish* starve

182   For the offense he dies. This is our doom.
         Some stay to see him fastened in the earth.

AARON
         Ah, why should wrath be mute and fury dumb?
         I am no baby, I, that with base prayers
         I should repent the evils I have done;
         Ten thousand worse than ever yet I did
         Would I perform if I might have my will.
         If one good deed in all my life I did,
190   I do repent it from my very soul.

LUCIUS
         Some loving friends convey the emperor hence,
         And give him burial in his father's grave.
         My father and Lavinia shall forthwith
         Be closèd in our household's monument.
         As for that ravenous tiger, Tamora,
         No funeral rite, nor man in mourning weeds,
         No mournful bell shall ring her burial;
         But throw her forth to beasts and birds to prey.
         Her life was beastly and devoid of pity,
200   And being dead, let birds on her take pity!   *Exeunt.*

---

182 *doom* sentence
   [201–4]
   See justice done on Aaron, that damned Moor,
   By whom our heavy haps had their beginning.
   Then, afterwards, to order well the state,
   That like events may ne'er it ruinate.
   (These lines, not included in Q1, were first printed in Q2. Since Q2 was
   printed from a defective copy of Q1, it appears that someone composed this
   passage in an effort to reconstruct the unreadable original.)